I0019029

Title of the Book
"The Science of Cybersecurity: Advanced Defense Techniq

Preface
In the digital age, cybersecurity is no longer an option but an absolute necessity. As threats grow increasingly sophisticated and emerge daily, understanding system vulnerabilities and mastering defense mechanisms have become critical skills for professionals. This book aims to serve as a comprehensive and advanced guide to the world of cybersecurity, blending theory, practical applications, and ethical hacking techniques to ensure robust protection.

Here, we delve deep into advanced attack and defense methodologies, moving far beyond the basics. Readers will explore not only types of malware and system vulnerabilities but also how to design, implement, and maintain resilient systems. Advanced techniques like penetration testing, digital forensic analysis, and reverse engineering are covered in detail, providing a holistic view of the cybersecurity landscape.

This book doesn't merely teach readers how to defend against threats; it also sheds light on how attackers think and operate. By understanding their strategies, it equips professionals with the tools needed to anticipate and prevent future attacks. The text is aimed at IT professionals, ethical hackers, advanced students, and anyone determined to build a secure and resilient digital ecosystem.

Index

Chapter 1: Evolution of Cybercrime - A Historical and Futuristic Overview

Introduction

Cybercrime is one of the most complex and pervasive phenomena of the digital age. As global communication networks and information technologies emerged, cybercrime evolved from sporadic and relatively simple activities to sophisticated operations carried out by organized groups, lone individuals, and even governments. This chapter examines the historical evolution of cybercrime, analyzing the techniques employed, the motivations of attackers, and the future challenges in cybersecurity

From the dawn of cybercrime in the 1970s to the present era dominated by ransomware, supply chain attacks, and malevolent artificial intelligence, this chapter demonstrates how technological progress has fueled this invisible yet omnipresent battle. Understanding the past and present of cybercrime is not merely a historical exercise but a strategic necessity to anticipate and address future threats.

1.1 The Dawn of Cybercrime
1.1.1 Origins of Cybercrime

Cybercrime began almost simultaneously with the advent of interconnected computing systems. In the 1970s, computers were primarily confined to government and academic institutions, and the concept of cybercrime was still rudimentary. However, the emergence of early networks marked the beginning of hacking activities, initially driven more by intellectual curiosity than malice.

The Creeper Virus (1971): Recognized as the first computer virus, the Creeper, created by Bob Thomas, was an experimental program that moved autonomously between systems. Though harmless, it highlighted the potential for self-replicating programs, laying the groundwork for future malicious software.
Early Software Piracy (1981): The Kildall brothers documented one of the first cases of software piracy, with illegal duplications of their CP/M operating system This marked the initial realization of digital vulnerabilities to unauthorized manipulation.
1.1.2 Early Motivations
The motivations behind early cyberattacks were often innocuous and exploratory. Hackers were driven by curiosity, a desire for notoriety, or an intellectual challenge.

Curiosity: Early hackers sought to understand the internal mechanisms of computing systems and expand their technical knowledge.
Academic Research: Many early incidents were tied to experiments conducted by students or researchers, often without harmful intent.
Intellectual Challenge: Systems were seen as puzzles to be solved, leading to unauthorized explorations.
Over time, as technology became more accessible and interconnected, cybercrime evolved into a profit-driven and malicious enterprise.

1.2 The Golden Age of Cybercrime
1.2.1 Emergence of Organized Cybercrime
With the proliferation of the internet in the 1990s, cybercrime transitioned into a global phenomenon. Organized crime syndicates recognized the potential of cyberspace for illicit activities, including identity theft, financial fraud, and malware distribution.

Phishing Scams: By the mid-1990s, phishing emails that mimicked legitimate entities began to surface. For instance, a 1996 campaign impersonated banks, luring victims into disclosing sensitive information, showcasing the psychological manipulation central to cybercrime.
1.2.2 Accessibility of Hacking Tools
During this era, hacking tools became widely available, democratizing cybercrime.

Even individuals with minimal expertise could execute attacks using software like keyloggers and trojan horses.

Keyloggers: These programs recorded keystrokes, enabling attackers to steal credentials.
Trojan Horses: Malicious programs disguised as useful applications allowed attackers to infiltrate systems undetected.
1.2.3 Landmark Incident: "I Love You" Worm (2000)
This infamous worm spread via email, infecting millions of computers globally and causing billions in damages. Its success stemmed from combining technical vulnerabilities with social engineering tactics, exploiting users' trust.

1.3 The Era of Globalized Cybercrime
1.3.1 Large-Scale Attacks
Entering the 2000s, cybercrime expanded to unprecedented scales. Distributed Denial of Service (DDoS) attacks became a prominent threat.

The Dyn Attack (2016): This DDoS assault targeted the DNS provider Dyn, disrupting major services like Twitter and Spotify. It highlighted the vulnerability of internet infrastructure to massive traffic overloads orchestrated by botnets.
1.3.2 The Rise of the Dark Web
The Dark Web revolutionized cybercrime by providing anonymous marketplaces like Silk Road and AlphaBay. These platforms facilitated the sale of stolen data, malware, and illegal services, making cybercrime more organized and accessible.

1.3.3 Supply Chain Attacks
Supply chain attacks emerged as one of the most sophisticated cybercrime techniques, targeting suppliers to infiltrate larger networks.

SolarWinds Hack (2020): This attack compromised thousands of organizations, including U.S. government agencies, by exploiting vulnerabilities in widely used software, demonstrating the dangers of interconnected ecosystems.
1.4 Modern Cybercrime: Motivations and Techniques
1.4.1 Evolving Motivations
Modern cybercrime encompasses diverse motivations:

Financial Profit: Cybercriminals primarily seek monetary gain through ransomware, phishing, and fraud.
Cyber Espionage: State-sponsored attackers aim to gather intelligence for geopolitical advantage.
Hacktivism: Groups like Anonymous conduct attacks to promote political or social causes.
1.4.2 Advanced Techniques
The sophistication of attacks has surged with new methodologies:

Ransomware as a Service (RaaS): This business model enables cybercriminals to rent ransomware tools for their operations.
Malicious AI: Artificial intelligence is used to craft personalized phishing emails and adaptive attacks, increasing their success rates.
1.5 A Glimpse into the Future
1.5.1 Emerging Threats
The future of cybercrime will likely introduce unprecedented challenges, including:

Deepfakes: These AI-generated synthetic media can be used for fraud and disinformation campaigns.
Quantum Computing: While promising breakthroughs, quantum computing may render current encryption methods obsolete, necessitating new defense strategies.
1.5.2 Future Defenses
To combat evolving threats, innovative strategies like Zero Trust Architecture

(ZTA) will become crucial. Moreover, global collaboration among governments, industries, and cybersecurity professionals will be essential to thwart future attacks.

Conclusion
This chapter provides a detailed exploration of cybercrime's evolution, from its origins to its current complexity. Understanding this progression is vital to tackling future challenges. In subsequent chapters, we will delve into types of malware, vulnerabilities, and advanced defense strategies, equipping readers with the tools to navigate the ever-changing landscape of cybercrime.

Chapter 2: Malware, Vulnerabilities, and System Hardening
Introduction
In the modern digital landscape, cybersecurity faces a relentless and escalating challenge: malware. These malicious software applications, coupled with system vulnerabilities, pose significant threats to individuals, enterprises, and governments alike. Tackling these threats requires a comprehensive understanding of the intricacies of malware, an awareness of the weaknesses inherent in systems, and the application of robust hardening techniques to fortify defenses.

This chapter provides a deep dive into the anatomy of malware, explores the vulnerabilities that hackers exploit, and discusses advanced strategies for hardening systems to minimize attack surfaces. By dissecting the various dimensions of these topics, this chapter arms cybersecurity professionals and ethical hackers with the knowledge and tools needed to anticipate, counteract, and mitigate threats effectively.

2.1 Understanding Malware: Types and Associated Threats
Malware, short for "malicious software," refers to a diverse category of programs designed to infiltrate, damage, or exploit computer systems. It encompasses a wide array of threats, each with distinct characteristics, delivery mechanisms, and attack objectives. A nuanced understanding of these types is critical to devising effective defensive strategies.

2.1.1 Viruses: The Foundational Threat
Viruses represent one of the oldest and most well-known forms of malware. First appearing in the early days of computing, these programs replicate themselves by embedding code into other files, spreading when the host file is executed. Their effects range from harmless pranks to catastrophic data loss.

Mechanics of a Virus:

Replication: Viruses propagate by inserting copies of themselves into executable files, boot sectors, or documents.
Trigger Mechanisms: Activation often requires user interaction, such as opening an infected attachment or executing a compromised program.
Effects: Depending on their design, viruses can disrupt operations, corrupt data, or render systems inoperable.
Case Study: The "ILOVEYOU" Virus In May 2000, the "ILOVEYOU" virus spread globally through email attachments disguised as love letters. Infecting millions of computers within hours, it overwrote files and caused billions of dollars in damages. Its rapid propagation demonstrated the dual danger of malicious code and human gullibility.

Defensive Measures:

Regular updates to antivirus software to detect and neutralize known virus signatures.
User education on the dangers of unsolicited email attachments.

Implementation of strict file execution policies to prevent unauthorized code from running.

2.1.2 Trojans: Disguised Invaders

Trojans take their name from the Greek tale of the Trojan horse, using deception to infiltrate systems. These malicious programs masquerade as legitimate software, tricking users into downloading and executing them.

How Trojans Work:

Camouflage: Often presented as utility tools, entertainment applications, or system updates.
Payloads: Once installed, Trojans may open backdoors, steal sensitive data, or deploy additional malware.
Delivery Mechanisms: Distributed via phishing emails, compromised websites, or rogue software downloads.
Case Study: The Zeus Trojan The Zeus Trojan targeted online banking users, employing keylogging to harvest login credentials. It enabled attackers to siphon millions from compromised accounts, highlighting the devastating impact of sophisticated Trojans.

Defense Strategies:

Employ behavioral analytics to identify anomalous software activities.
Maintain strict controls over software installations, allowing only verified applications.
Educate users on recognizing phishing attempts and avoiding unofficial download sources.

2.1.3 Worms: Self-Propagating Threats

Worms distinguish themselves by their ability to spread autonomously across networks, requiring no host file or user action. Their independence and speed make them particularly dangerous.

Characteristics of Worms:

Autonomous Propagation: Worms exploit vulnerabilities in network protocols or software to spread.
Resource Consumption: They can overwhelm networks by generating excessive traffic.
Potential for Destruction: Worms may deliver malicious payloads or disrupt critical services.
Case Study: The Conficker Worm Detected in 2008, the Conficker worm exploited a vulnerability in Windows systems, infecting millions of devices. It disrupted business operations, highlighting the importance of timely patch management.

Mitigation Techniques:

Apply software patches promptly to eliminate known vulnerabilities.
Use firewalls and intrusion detection systems to monitor network traffic.
Segment networks to contain the spread of infections.

2.1.4 Ransomware: Digital Extortionists

Ransomware encrypts victims' files, rendering them inaccessible until a ransom is paid. Its profitability has led to a surge in ransomware attacks, often targeting businesses and critical infrastructure.

Key Features:

Encryption: Advanced algorithms lock data, demanding decryption keys.
Payment Demands: Ransom payments are usually required in cryptocurrencies to ensure anonymity.
Distribution: Commonly spread through phishing campaigns or vulnerable systems.

Case Study: WannaCry In 2017, the WannaCry ransomware exploited a vulnerability in Windows systems, encrypting data on over 200,000 devices worldwide. Its global reach and significant impact underscored the importance of proactive defense.

Protective Measures:

Regularly back up data and store copies offline.
Deploy endpoint detection and response (EDR) tools to identify ransomware activity.
Conduct employee training to recognize phishing schemes.
2.1.5 Spyware and Adware: Silent Threats
Spyware and adware are less overtly destructive but equally insidious. Spyware secretly collects user data, while adware bombards users with unwanted advertisements.

Mechanisms of Operation:

Spyware: Gathers information such as browsing habits, login credentials, or financial data.
Adware: Displays intrusive ads, often redirecting users to malicious sites.
Case Study: Pegasus Spyware The Pegasus spyware was capable of infecting devices without user interaction, harvesting vast amounts of sensitive data undetected.

Preventative Steps:

Use robust anti-spyware tools to monitor and block unauthorized data collection.
Configure browsers to block pop-ups and third-party trackers.
Restrict software installations to reputable sources.
2.2 Vulnerabilities: Exploitable Weaknesses
Vulnerabilities in systems are the gateways through which malware operates. These weaknesses may stem from flawed software, improper configurations, or human errors.

Common Causes:
Outdated Software: Unpatched systems leave exploitable gaps.
Misconfigurations: Default settings or insufficient access controls create openings for attackers.
Human Error: Phishing and other social engineering techniques capitalize on user mistakes.
2.3 Hardening Systems: Strengthening Defenses
Hardening a system involves reducing its attack surface and implementing multiple layers of security to mitigate vulnerabilities.

2.3.1 Principles of Hardening
Surface Reduction: Disable unnecessary services, applications, and ports to minimize exposure.
Timely Updates: Regularly apply security patches and updates to close known vulnerabilities.
Configuration Management: Establish strict controls for access permissions, firewall rules, and password policies.
2.3.2 Hardening Tools
Microsoft Security Baseline: Provides pre-configured security settings for Windows systems.
SELinux (Security-Enhanced Linux): Implements mandatory access controls to protect sensitive resources.
Firewalls: Solutions like pfSense and iptables allow precise traffic regulation, preventing unauthorized access.
Conclusion
This chapter has explored the multifaceted world of malware, the vulnerabilities they exploit, and the hardening strategies necessary to build resilient systems. By integrating comprehensive defenses with a proactive approach, cybersecurity

rofessionals can significantly reduce risks and fortify systems against evolving threats. The next chapters will delve deeper into advanced defense mechanisms and ethical hacking techniques, equipping readers with the expertise to counteract the ever-changing cyber threat landscape.

Chapter 3: Cybercrime and Ransomware – Understanding and Countering the Threats

Introduction

The advent of modern technology has birthed a new frontier for criminal activity: cybercrime. Unlike traditional crime, cybercrime exploits computers, networks, and digital systems as its primary tools for theft, fraud, extortion, and sabotage. Among the most destructive threats within this domain is ransomware, a type of malware designed to encrypt a victim's data and demand payment for its release.

This chapter offers an in-depth exploration of the landscape of cybercrime and ransomware, delving into their evolution, operational mechanisms, and advanced countermeasures. By understanding these threats and their pervasive impact, cybersecurity professionals and organizations can better prepare for and defend against the complexities of the digital criminal world.

3.1 The Realm of Cybercrime

Cybercrime has emerged as a global phenomenon, continuously evolving in scale and sophistication. Its implications reach far beyond individual victims, impacting governments, businesses, and societies. To counteract cybercrime effectively, it is essential to understand its manifestations, categories, and organized structures.

3.1.1 Primary Categories of Cybercrime

Cybercrime encompasses a variety of malicious activities, each with unique methodologies and objectives. Key categories include:

1. Hacking and Cyberattacks

Definition and Methods: Hacking involves unauthorized access to systems, networks, or devices. Motivations range from stealing information to causing operational disruptions.
Techniques:
Exploiting software vulnerabilities, such as buffer overflows or SQL injections.
Employing social engineering tactics to manipulate users into revealing credentials.
Case Study: The 2014 Sony Pictures hack exposed sensitive emails, unreleased films, and confidential corporate data, causing financial and reputational damage.
2. Online Fraud and Phishing

Mechanism: Fraudulent emails, websites, or messages designed to deceive individuals into disclosing personal or financial information.
Advanced Tactics: Spear-phishing targets specific individuals or organizations with personalized messages that appear legitimate.
Impact: Phishing scams account for billions in financial losses annually and often serve as the gateway for broader attacks.
3. Financial Crimes

Tools: Banking trojans and other malware are employed to access accounts and facilitate unauthorized fund transfers.
Example: Emotet, initially a banking trojan, evolved into a sophisticated malware delivery platform, enabling complex cyberattacks.
4. Identity Theft

Methods: Using spyware, keyloggers, or database breaches to collect personal data, which is then used to impersonate victims for financial or social harm.
Consequences: Victims may suffer financial losses, damaged reputations, and

prolonged recovery efforts.
5. Attacks on Critical Infrastructure

Targets: Power grids, water systems, hospitals, and other essential services.
Significance: These attacks pose risks to public safety and national security.
Example: In 2021, a ransomware attack on Colonial Pipeline disrupted fuel supplies
across the United States, demonstrating the far-reaching consequences of such
breaches.
3.1.2 The Rise of Organized Cybercrime
Beyond individual hackers, many cybercrimes are orchestrated by structured groups
operating like legitimate businesses. These organizations leverage economies of
scale and technological expertise to expand their reach.

1. As-a-Service Models

Ransomware-as-a-Service (RaaS): Professional-grade ransomware kits sold or leased
to less skilled attackers.
Impact: Lowers the barrier to entry, enabling more widespread attacks.
2. Dark Web Marketplaces

Offerings: Malware, stolen credentials, exploit kits, and other cybercrime tools
are sold anonymously.
Role in Cybercrime: These marketplaces foster collaboration and innovation among
criminals, amplifying the threat landscape.
3.1.3 Consequences of Cybercrime
Cybercrime impacts every facet of modern life, manifesting in various ways:

Economic Costs: Direct financial losses, costs of system recovery, and reputationa
damage.
Social Impact: Erosion of trust in digital ecosystems and psychological harm to
victims.
Political Repercussions: Electoral interference, industrial espionage, and
destabilization of international relations.
3.2 Ransomware: The New Face of Digital Crime
Ransomware has emerged as one of the most severe cybersecurity threats,
characterized by its rapid evolution and increasing sophistication. Understanding
its nature, types, and propagation methods is vital to countering this menace.

3.2.1 What is Ransomware?
Ransomware is a form of malware designed to encrypt a victim's files, rendering
them inaccessible until a ransom is paid. Its technical sophistication and
profitability make it a preferred weapon for cybercriminals.

Technical Mechanisms:
Uses encryption algorithms like AES and RSA to lock files.
Often combines multiple encryption layers to complicate recovery efforts.
Payment Methods:
Typically demands cryptocurrency transactions to ensure anonymity.
3.2.2 Types of Ransomware
Ransomware varies in functionality and objectives, falling into distinct
categories:

Locker Ransomware:

Locks victims out of their devices without encrypting files.
Commonly targets smartphones or unsophisticated systems.
Example: Android/Simplocker.
Crypto Ransomware:

Encrypts files, making them inaccessible without a decryption key.
Example: WannaCry, which exploited a Windows vulnerability in 2017, causing widespread disruption.
Double Extortion Ransomware:

Encrypts data and threatens to publish it online if the ransom is not paid.
Example: Maze ransomware pioneered this tactic, increasing the pressure on victims.

3.2.3 Methods of Distribution
Ransomware leverages various vectors to reach its targets:

Phishing Emails: Deceptive emails containing infected attachments or links.
Exploitation of Vulnerabilities: Leveraging software flaws, such as the EternalBlue exploit used in WannaCry.
Brute Force Attacks: Guessing weak passwords to gain unauthorized access.
Drive-By Downloads: Infecting users via malicious websites.

3.2.4 Notable Ransomware Cases
Petya/NotPetya: Initially a ransomware variant, it evolved into a destructive wiper malware.
REvil: A high-profile group known for targeting large corporations and demanding multimillion-dollar ransoms.

3.3 Advanced Defense Strategies
Combating ransomware and cybercrime requires a layered defense approach, combining prevention, incident response, and system hardening.

3.3.1 Prevention
Regular Backups: Store backup copies offline to prevent ransomware from encrypting them.
Advanced Security Tools: Use Endpoint Detection and Response (EDR) solutions to monitor and mitigate threats in real time.
Patch Management: Keep all software and systems updated to close vulnerabilities.
User Education: Train employees to recognize phishing emails and other social engineering tactics.

3.3.2 Incident Response
System Isolation: Disconnect infected systems from networks to limit the spread of ransomware.
Incident Analysis: Identify the type of ransomware and trace the infection path.
Expert Consultation: Engage cybersecurity specialists or law enforcement for support.
Avoid Paying the Ransom: Payment encourages further attacks and does not guarantee data recovery.

3.3.3 Hardening Techniques
Network Segmentation: Use firewalls and VLANs to isolate critical systems.
Zero Trust Architecture: Assume all users and devices are untrusted until verified.
Multi-Factor Authentication (MFA): Add an extra layer of security to access controls.

Conclusion
Cybercrime and ransomware continue to evolve, posing significant risks to individuals, businesses, and governments. However, with a combination of awareness, advanced technologies, and proactive defense strategies, these threats can be effectively mitigated. Future chapters will delve deeper into cutting-edge techniques for tackling these challenges, empowering cybersecurity professionals to safeguard systems in an increasingly hostile digital environment.

Chapter 4: Spyware and Adware – Silent Threats to Privacy and Security
Introduction
Spyware and adware, while less catastrophic than other malware types like ransomware or trojans, represent a significant and pervasive threat to privacy and security. These software forms can infiltrate systems, disrupt user experiences, and compromise sensitive data. Spyware is designed to covertly monitor and gather

personal information, often for malicious purposes, whereas adware floods devices with intrusive advertisements that can degrade performance and redirect users to unsafe websites. In this chapter, we explore the intricacies of spyware and adware, their mechanisms, propagation methods, detection techniques, and advanced strategies for prevention and removal. Additionally, the chapter delves into their implications for personal privacy and broader cybersecurity landscapes, providing professionals with a comprehensive understanding of these threats.

4.1 Spyware: An Invisible Threat

Spyware represents one of the stealthiest forms of malware, designed to monitor and extract sensitive user information without their knowledge. Its discreet nature and adaptability make it particularly insidious, posing risks to both individuals and organizations.

4.1.1 Characteristics and Functionality of Spyware

Spyware operates by embedding itself into systems to gather data and send it to third parties. This data can include anything from browsing histories to highly sensitive financial information or login credentials. Its ability to remain undetected allows attackers to extract information over extended periods, maximizing the potential damage.

Key Characteristics:

Data Collection: Spyware targets personal and sensitive data such as passwords, PINs, and credit card details. Some types, like keyloggers, record every keystroke, providing attackers with unfiltered access to user inputs.

Covert Operation: Spyware often operates silently, avoiding detection by disguising itself as legitimate software or integrating into system processes. Advanced spyware uses rootkits or other cloaking techniques to evade antivirus tools.

Impact:

Violates user privacy by exposing sensitive information.
Facilitates identity theft and financial fraud.
Compromises system security, enabling broader cyberattacks.

4.1.2 Types of Spyware

Spyware comes in various forms, each with specific functions tailored to its intended goals:

Keyloggers:

Purpose: Record keystrokes to capture passwords, bank credentials, and personal information.
Example: Malicious keyloggers have been deployed in targeted attacks against corporate executives to steal trade secrets.
Trojan Spyware:

Purpose: Masquerades as legitimate software, tricking users into installation. Once installed, it begins monitoring activities and transmitting data to attackers.
Example: Emotet, originally a banking trojan, evolved into a sophisticated malware platform, targeting high-value organizations for data exfiltration.
Commercial Spyware:

Purpose: Often marketed as employee monitoring tools but used for unethical surveillance.
Risks: Violates privacy laws and ethical boundaries, especially when deployed without informed consent.
Tracking Cookies:

Purpose: While technically less harmful, they track online behavior to create user profiles for targeted advertising.
Risks: These profiles can be misused, exposing users to privacy breaches.

4.1.3 How Spyware Propagates

Spyware employs multiple vectors for dissemination:

Malicious Downloads:

Fake or pirated software often contains embedded spyware.
Users inadvertently install spyware by downloading free software from unreliable sources.
Phishing Campaigns:

Deceptive emails or messages trick users into clicking malicious links or attachments.
Exploiting Software Vulnerabilities:

Outdated systems and applications provide entry points for spyware.
Bundled Installations:

Legitimate-looking applications may bundle spyware, installing it alongside useful features.

4.2 Adware: Invasive Advertising and Secondary Risks

Adware, though often perceived as less harmful, can significantly disrupt user experiences while posing potential security risks.

4.2.1 Characteristics of Adware

Adware delivers advertisements, often through intrusive means such as pop-ups, banners, or redirect links. While some forms of adware may seem benign, others collect user data or redirect traffic to malicious sites.

Key Characteristics:

Resource Consumption: Adware slows system performance by monopolizing resources to generate and display advertisements.
Data Collection: Adware often tracks user activities to build detailed profiles, which are sold to advertisers or used to target individuals with customized ads.
Impact:

Erodes user experience with constant interruptions.
Creates entry points for additional malware infections.
Can lead to security breaches if users interact with malicious ads.

4.3 Advanced Detection Techniques

Spyware and adware are challenging to detect due to their ability to blend into legitimate system processes. However, advanced techniques can help uncover their presence.

4.3.1 Behavioral Analysis

Monitoring system behavior for anomalies, such as unusual network activity or unexplained CPU spikes, helps identify spyware and adware.
Example: An unknown process transmitting large volumes of data to an unfamiliar server could indicate spyware.

4.3.2 Heuristic Analysis

Analyzes file structures for irregularities that suggest malicious intent.
Tools like Sysmon and Wireshark can provide forensic insights into network activity and system processes.

4.3.3 Network Traffic Monitoring

Examines outgoing connections for suspicious activity, such as communication with

known malicious IPs.
Packet analysis can reveal spyware attempting to exfiltrate data.
4.4 Prevention and Removal Strategies
Proactively defending against spyware and adware requires robust security measures, while effective removal techniques ensure clean systems post-infection.

4.4.1 Prevention
Use of Security Tools:

Install and regularly update antivirus and anti-spyware software.
Enable real-time protection features.
System Updates:

Regularly apply patches to operating systems and applications to close security vulnerabilities.
Safe Browsing Practices:

Avoid clicking on unsolicited links or downloading files from untrusted sources.
Access Controls:

Restrict user permissions to prevent unauthorized installations.
4.4.2 Removal
Detection Tools:

Applications like Malwarebytes or AdwCleaner are specifically designed to identify and remove spyware and adware.
Restoration:

For heavily infected systems, restoring to a previous clean state may be necessary.
Forensic Analysis:

Perform a detailed examination to ensure complete removal and to understand the infection's origin.
4.5 Privacy and Security Implications
Both spyware and adware undermine privacy by collecting and exploiting user data. Spyware, in particular, can cause severe consequences like identity theft and financial losses. Adware, while often underestimated, facilitates additional malware infections and erodes trust in digital systems.

These threats underscore the necessity of robust cybersecurity practices. Education, coupled with advanced detection and prevention strategies, is vital in safeguarding personal and organizational security.

Conclusion
Spyware and adware are pervasive threats that demand attention in any comprehensive cybersecurity strategy. By understanding their characteristics, propagation methods, and the tools available for detection and removal, professionals can effectively combat these threats. A proactive approach that combines prevention, education, and advanced technological defenses ensures a secure digital environment, preserving both privacy and operational integrity.

Chapter 5: Combating Malware – Advanced Strategies and Defense Techniques
Introduction
Malware is one of the most pervasive and evolving threats in the cybersecurity landscape. Combating it requires not just awareness of the latest attack methods but also the application of multi-layered defense strategies that integrate advanced technologies, rigorous training, and a proactive approach to system management. This chapter delves deep into sophisticated methodologies for defending against malware, expanding on the key elements of detection, prevention,

mitigation, and recovery. Each section provides an exhaustive exploration to equip security professionals and ethical hackers with a robust understanding of the principles and practices necessary to secure systems effectively.

5.1 Installing Antivirus and Antimalware Software

5.1.1 The Foundation of Defense

Antivirus and antimalware software are the cornerstone of any defense strategy against malware. These tools are designed to:

Detect and neutralize threats in real-time.
Provide periodic scans to uncover dormant or hidden malware.
Deliver updates to tackle emerging threats.

5.1.2 The Evolution of Malware Detection

Modern antivirus solutions utilize a variety of advanced techniques:

Signature-Based Detection: This traditional method relies on a database of known malware signatures. While effective for well-documented threats, its inability to recognize novel or polymorphic malware underscores the need for supplemental technologies.

Behavioral Analysis: Unlike signature-based methods, behavioral analysis evaluates the actions of programs to identify suspicious activities, such as unauthorized data exfiltration or system modifications.

Heuristic Analysis: This technique examines code structures and execution patterns to flag anomalies. It is particularly useful for identifying previously unseen malware variants.

AI and Machine Learning: The integration of artificial intelligence (AI) has revolutionized malware detection. Machine learning models analyze vast datasets to identify subtle patterns associated with malware, enabling the prediction and mitigation of threats even before they materialize fully.

5.1.3 Optimizing Antivirus Deployment

Proper configuration and maintenance of antivirus software ensure maximum efficacy:

Real-Time Protection: Enable continuous monitoring of file transfers, email attachments, and network traffic.
Scheduled Scans: Regular scans can identify dormant threats missed by real-time monitoring.
Cloud-Integrated Solutions: Cloud-based systems can provide quicker updates and access to global threat intelligence.

5.1.4 Challenges and Limitations

Despite its importance, antivirus software has limitations:

It cannot guarantee protection against zero-day exploits.
Advanced persistent threats (APTs) often evade detection by blending into legitimate processes.

5.2 Regular System and Software Updates

5.2.1 The Role of Updates in Security

Regular updates to operating systems and software are critical in closing security gaps. Vulnerabilities, when left unpatched, provide an open door for attackers.

5.2.2 Real-World Consequences

The WannaCry ransomware attack demonstrated the catastrophic impact of neglecting updates. The exploit leveraged a vulnerability in Windows, despite the availability of a patch months prior. Organizations and individuals who failed to update their systems became prime targets.

5.2.3 Implementing Patch Management
Effective patch management involves:

Vulnerability Assessment: Regularly scan systems to identify outdated software and prioritize patches based on severity.
Controlled Rollout: Test updates in sandbox environments before deploying them across production systems.
Automation Tools: Utilize automated patch management solutions to ensure timely an consistent application.

5.2.4 Overcoming Update Challenges
Organizations often face obstacles such as system downtime during updates or compatibility issues. A phased update approach, coupled with thorough testing, can mitigate these risks.

5.3 Using Legitimate Software and Trusted Sources
5.3.1 The Risks of Illegitimate Software
Downloading software from untrusted sources significantly increases the risk of malware infections. Common threats include:

Trojan Horses: Malicious software disguised as legitimate applications.
Keyloggers: Embedded in pirated software, these tools record keystrokes to steal sensitive information.

5.3.2 Best Practices for Software Acquisition
Rely on Official Sources: Always download software from the developer's official website or verified platforms.
Verify Digital Signatures: Ensure downloaded files are signed by a reputable developer.
Utilize Software Whitelisting: Employ tools that allow only pre-approved software to run, preventing unauthorized installations.

5.3.3 Educating Users
Educating users about the dangers of unverified software is critical. Practical training and awareness campaigns can help them make informed decisions when downloading applications.

5.4 User Education and Awareness
5.4.1 The Human Factor in Cybersecurity
Even the most advanced defenses can be compromised by user error. Phishing attacks in particular, exploit human psychology to bypass technical safeguards.

5.4.2 Designing Effective Training Programs
Recognizing Threats: Teach users to identify phishing attempts by analyzing:

Sender authenticity.
Grammar and spelling errors.
Unusual requests for sensitive information.
Interactive Training Modules: Utilize simulations and gamified learning to engage users and reinforce critical skills.

Continuous Learning: Update training programs regularly to address new threat vectors, such as spear-phishing or deepfake scams.

5.4.3 Measuring Effectiveness
Periodic testing through simulated attacks can assess user awareness and identify areas for improvement.

5.5 Implementing Comprehensive Security Policies
5.5.1 Defining Security Frameworks
Security policies establish the foundation for organizational cybersecurity. Key components include:

Access Control: Define roles and restrict access based on necessity.
Password Management: Mandate the use of strong, unique passwords and multi-factor authentication (MFA).

5.5.2 Incident Response Protocols
An effective incident response plan outlines:

Detection: Identifying breaches promptly.
Containment: Isolating affected systems to prevent further spread.
Recovery: Restoring operations and implementing lessons learned.

5.5.3 Policy Enforcement
Regular audits and compliance checks ensure adherence to security policies. Tools like SIEM (Security Information and Event Management) systems can automate this process.

5.6 Backup and Recovery
5.6.1 Designing Resilient Backup Strategies
Backup systems should be:

Comprehensive: Include all critical data, applications, and configurations.
Secure: Use encryption to protect backup data.
Redundant: Store backups across multiple locations, including offline and cloud storage.

5.6.2 Testing Recovery Procedures
Regular testing ensures backups are functional and recovery processes are efficient. Simulated disaster recovery exercises can validate the organization's preparedness.

5.6.3 Aligning with Business Continuity Plans
Integrating backup and recovery with broader business continuity strategies ensures minimal disruption during incidents.

Conclusion
Defending against malware requires an advanced and multifaceted approach. From cutting-edge technologies like AI-powered antivirus solutions to the fundamental practice of regular updates, each element of a defense strategy plays a vital role. User education, policy enforcement, and robust backup systems complement these efforts, creating a comprehensive framework for malware mitigation. By adopting these advanced strategies, cybersecurity professionals and ethical hackers can build resilient systems capable of withstanding even the most sophisticated threats.

Chapter 6: Monitoring Processes in Windows and Linux – Advanced Techniques and Optimal Practices
Introduction
Process monitoring is a fundamental component of system management and cybersecurity. It ensures that systems operate efficiently, detects potential security threats, and aids in troubleshooting performance issues. Both Windows and Linux provide a plethora of tools and methods for tracking, analyzing, and managing processes. Mastering these tools is crucial for IT professionals and ethical hackers who aim to secure environments against evolving threats.

This chapter provides an in-depth exploration of advanced monitoring techniques, delving into tools, strategies, and best practices for process management on Windows and Linux. Each point is expanded with comprehensive explanations, real-world applications, and practical examples to maximize understanding and utility.

Monitoring Processes in Windows
6.1 Processes in Windows: Fundamentals

A process in Windows is an instance of a running program. Each process has its own memory space and threads that perform specific tasks. Monitoring these processes helps identify abnormal behavior, optimize system performance, and ensure operational integrity.

6.2 Task Manager: Basic Monitoring
The Task Manager is the built-in tool for monitoring processes in Windows. It provides a quick overview of:

Running processes: Applications, background processes, and system tasks.
Resource usage: CPU, memory, disk, and network utilization.
Startup impact: Programs that run at system boot and their performance impact.
While Task Manager is sufficient for basic monitoring, it has limitations in diagnosing complex issues. For example, it doesn't reveal hidden processes or offer detailed insights into thread-level activities.

Use Case:

A system administrator notices system slowdown. Task Manager reveals an unfamiliar process consuming excessive CPU. By right-clicking on the process, they open its location, identifying it as malware. This quick action prevents further system compromise.
6.3 Process Explorer: Advanced Analysis
Process Explorer, part of the Microsoft Sysinternals Suite, is a powerful alternative to Task Manager. It provides detailed information about:

Parent-child relationships between processes.
Loaded DLLs and open file handles.
Process execution paths and digital signature verification.
Example Application: A suspicious process named explorer.exe is detected. Using Process Explorer:

The administrator inspects its file path and finds it in an unusual directory (not C:\Windows\System32).
A signature check reveals it is unsigned malware.
The administrator terminates the process and deletes the malicious file, stopping the threat.
Process Explorer also allows real-time monitoring of CPU and memory usage, enabling the identification of bottlenecks or malicious activity.

6.4 Windows Management Instrumentation (WMI): Automation and Precision
WMI is a framework for managing and monitoring Windows systems through scripting or command-line interfaces like PowerShell. It enables deep system insights and automation of routine tasks.

Key WMI Commands:

Get-Process: Lists running processes with their resource usage.
Get-WmiObject Win32_Process: Provides detailed process properties, such as command-line arguments and start times.
Example: A PowerShell script uses WMI to log processes consuming more than 80% of CPU:

```powershell
Copy code
Get-WmiObject Win32_Process | Where-Object { $_.PercentProcessorTime -gt 80 }
```
This script automates resource monitoring, sending alerts when thresholds are exceeded.

6.5 Event Viewer: Logging and Investigation

The Event Viewer logs critical system events, including:

Process creation and termination (Event ID 4688).
Security incidents, such as unauthorized access attempts.
Application errors that could indicate malware activity.
Scenario: A malware program creates multiple hidden processes. Event Viewer logs these under specific event IDs, enabling administrators to trace the malware's entry point and propagation.

Monitoring Processes in Linux

6.6 Processes in Linux: Overview

In Linux, processes are integral to system functionality, each managed by the kernel. Every process is assigned a unique Process ID (PID), facilitating targeted analysis and management.

6.7 The top and htop Utilities: Real-Time Insights

top is a command-line tool for real-time monitoring of:

Resource usage by processes (CPU, memory, etc.).
System load averages.
Process priorities and statuses.
htop enhances top by offering:

A user-friendly, color-coded interface.
Interactive controls for process termination or priority adjustment.
Enhanced sorting and filtering options.
Example: An administrator identifies a process consuming 95% of CPU resources using htop. They terminate the process or adjust its priority using renice, restoring system stability.

6.8 The ps Command: Static Snapshots

The ps command provides static snapshots of all running processes. Combined with filters, it becomes a powerful diagnostic tool.

Key Commands:

ps aux: Lists all processes with detailed attributes (user, PID, CPU, memory usage).
ps aux | grep <process_name>: Filters processes by name or attributes.
Scenario: To identify all processes owned by a specific user, the administrator executes:

```bash
Copy code
ps aux | grep username
```
This reveals unauthorized processes running under the user's account.

6.9 Advanced Tools: strace and lsof

strace: This tool traces system calls made by a process, offering visibility into its interactions with the operating system.

Use Case: Tracing file access by a suspected malicious process:

```bash
Copy code
strace -e open -p <PID>
```
lsof: Lists open files and network connections used by processes, enabling identification of suspicious activity.

Example: A process maintaining a persistent connection to an unknown IP address is flagged by lsof. The administrator blocks the connection and investigates the process further.

6.10 Threat Detection Through Process Monitoring
6.10.1 Windows Techniques
Behavioral Analysis: Processes consuming unusually high CPU or memory are flagged for further inspection.
Signature Verification: Using Process Explorer, unsigned or fake-signed processes are identified and terminated.
Event Logging: Analyzing logs in Event Viewer reveals anomalies in process creation patterns.
6.10.2 Linux Techniques
Rootkit Detection: Tools like chkrootkit and rkhunter scan for hidden malicious processes.
Network Analysis: Monitoring outbound connections with Wireshark or tcpdump detects processes communicating with Command and Control (C&C) servers.
6.11 Best Practices for Process Monitoring
6.11.1 Automated Alerts
Set up alerts for suspicious activities, such as:

High resource consumption by a single process.
Unauthorized access to sensitive files or directories.
6.11.2 Sandboxing
Use sandbox environments like Cuckoo Sandbox to safely analyze suspicious files and processes without risking the main system.

6.11.3 Audit Trails
Implement tools like auditd in Linux to maintain detailed logs of system activities, helping trace malicious actions or policy violations.

Conclusion
Process monitoring is a vital aspect of system security and performance optimization. Whether on Windows or Linux, mastering the tools and techniques outlined in this chapter equips administrators and ethical hackers with the skills to detect, analyze, and neutralize threats effectively. By combining proactive monitoring, automated alerts, and behavioral analysis, you can ensure a secure and efficient operating environment.

Chapter 7: Hardening the Operating System – Advanced Approaches and Defense Techniques
Introduction
The operating system (OS) serves as the core of any IT infrastructure, acting as the central hub for managing hardware, applications, and system resources. Its security is paramount because vulnerabilities within the OS can lead to widespread system compromise. Hardening the OS involves systematically securing configurations, removing unnecessary components, and implementing advanced defenses to minimize potential attack surfaces.

This chapter delves into comprehensive hardening techniques for Windows and Linux, detailing advanced strategies, best practices, and real-world examples to meet the security needs of modern, complex environments.

Understanding OS Hardening
The primary objective of OS hardening is to reduce the attack surface—the sum of all possible entry points that an attacker could exploit. Achieving this goal involves a multi-faceted approach:

1. Removing Unnecessary Services and Applications

Every active service or installed application represents a potential vulnerability. By identifying and disabling or uninstalling those that are unnecessary, you can significantly reduce risks.

Why It's Critical: Attackers often exploit vulnerabilities in rarely used services, especially default installations.

Best Practices:
Conduct a thorough audit to identify unneeded services or software.
In Windows, use Task Manager and Services to review running processes. For Linux, use:

```bash
Copy code
systemctl list-units --type=service
```

to identify active services.
Document dependencies before disabling services to ensure critical functionality is not disrupted.

2. Implementing Secure Configurations

OS configurations influence how the system manages resources and interacts with users. Insecure configurations can provide attackers with avenues to exploit the system.

Examples:
Ensure unused ports are closed.
Restrict file and folder permissions to only authorized users.
Configure system policies to enforce stringent password requirements.

Implementation:
Use configuration management tools like Ansible or Puppet to automate secure settings across multiple systems.
Leverage benchmarks like the CIS Benchmarks for system-specific best practices.

3. Patch Management

Patches address known vulnerabilities, often fixing critical security flaws. Failure to apply patches can leave systems exposed.

Notable Example: The WannaCry ransomware exploited a known vulnerability in SMB on Windows systems, which had a patch available but was not widely applied.

Best Practices:
Schedule regular patch reviews and updates.
Test patches in a staging environment before deployment.
Use tools like WSUS (Windows Server Update Services) or a Linux package manager (apt, yum) to automate updates.

Advanced Hardening Techniques for Windows Operating Systems
Windows systems are often targeted due to their widespread use. Hardening Windows OS requires addressing vulnerabilities at multiple levels, including registry settings, user account management, and built-in tools.

1. Securing the Windows Registry

The Windows Registry is a central database that stores configuration settings. Incorrect or insecure settings can expose the system to attacks.

Advanced Hardening:
Use the Group Policy Editor to enforce security policies. For example, prevent executable files from running in temporary directories:

```
Copy code
HKLM\Software\Policies\Microsoft\Windows\AppLocker
```

Implement auditing on sensitive keys to monitor unauthorized changes.
Best Practice: Regularly back up the registry to ensure a quick rollback in case of corruption or an attack.

2. Enhancing User Account Protection

Accounts with excessive privileges pose significant risks, especially if compromised. Minimizing these privileges is key.

Techniques:
Use Multi-Factor Authentication (MFA) for all administrator accounts.
Enable Account Lockout Policies to prevent brute-force attacks.
Disable or rename the default Administrator account to prevent targeted attacks.
Example: Implement role-based access control (RBAC) in Active Directory to ensure users can access only what they need.
3. Configuring Windows Firewall
The built-in Windows Defender Firewall provides robust tools for controlling network traffic.

Advanced Configuration:
Define custom inbound and outbound rules to allow only necessary traffic.
Use predefined profiles (domain, private, public) to restrict traffic based on network location.
Practical Application:
Block outbound traffic for applications that should not access the internet, reducing the risk of data exfiltration.
4. Activating and Managing BitLocker
BitLocker encrypts data at rest, protecting sensitive information from unauthorized access.

Advanced Use:
Integrate BitLocker management with Active Directory to enforce organization-wide policies.
Enable pre-boot authentication for an additional layer of protection.
Advanced Hardening Techniques for Linux Operating Systems
Linux is widely used in server environments and requires specialized techniques for effective hardening.

1. Configuring File Permissions
Linux's hierarchical permission system ensures that users, groups, and others have controlled access to files and directories.

Advanced Hardening:
Use the umask setting to enforce restrictive default permissions.
Regularly audit sensitive files like /etc/passwd and /etc/shadow to ensure their integrity.
Best Practice:
bash
Copy code

```
chmod 600 /etc/ssh/sshd_config
```

This restricts the SSH configuration file to root access only.
2. Securing SSH Access
Secure Shell (SSH) is a vital service, but improper configurations can leave systems exposed.

Advanced Techniques:
Disable password authentication, relying on key-based authentication:
perl
Copy code

```
PasswordAuthentication no
```

Restrict SSH to specific users by editing /etc/ssh/sshd_config:
Copy code

```
AllowUsers admin user1
```

Example: Use tools like Fail2ban to block IPs with multiple failed login attempts.
3. Using SELinux and AppArmor

These tools enforce mandatory access control (MAC) policies, providing granular control over application behavior.

SELinux:
Configure custom policies to isolate applications, limiting their access to the file system and network resources.
AppArmor:
Use predefined profiles to restrict application behavior and minimize risk.
4. Disabling Unnecessary Services
Active services increase the potential attack surface.

Best Practices:
Use:
bash
Copy code
```
systemctl disable <service_name>
```
to prevent unnecessary services from starting at boot.
Regularly review active services with:
perl
Copy code
```
ps aux | grep service
```
Best Practices for OS Hardening
1. Patch and Update Policies
Automate updates where possible but ensure proper testing to avoid introducing new issues.

Example: Use yum-cron on Linux for automatic updates while retaining manual control over critical patches.
2. Regular Backups
Frequent and secure backups are crucial, especially in environments prone to ransomware attacks.

Advanced Practice:
Implement incremental backups to minimize storage requirements.
Use encrypted backups to ensure data security.
3. Continuous Monitoring
Monitoring ensures that threats and anomalies are detected promptly.

Tools:
Nagios: Monitors system health and resource usage.
Splunk: Analyzes logs for suspicious activity.
Example: Configure alerts for unusual CPU or network usage, which could indicate an ongoing attack.
4. Security Testing
Regular vulnerability assessments help identify weaknesses before attackers can exploit them.

Example: Use OpenVAS or Nessus to scan for misconfigurations and unpatched vulnerabilities.
Follow up scans with remediation efforts and repeat tests to validate fixes.
Conclusion
Operating system hardening is a cornerstone of IT security, providing the foundation for a resilient and secure infrastructure. While the techniques outlined in this chapter form a comprehensive framework for both Windows and Linux systems, the process must remain dynamic, adapting to new threats and evolving technologies.

By combining advanced configurations, proactive monitoring, and regular testing, IT professionals can ensure the integrity, availability, and confidentiality of their operating systems, safeguarding the critical infrastructures they support.

Chapter 8: Hardening Network Devices – Strengthening the Foundations of Security

Introduction

Network devices, such as routers, switches, firewalls, and wireless access points, form the critical backbone of any IT infrastructure. These devices are responsible for managing traffic, regulating access, and protecting vital data. However, their central role and complexity make them prime targets for cyberattacks. The process of hardening these devices—fortifying their configurations and implementing security measures—is essential to minimize risks and ensure the stability and security of the network.

This chapter provides an in-depth exploration of advanced techniques for hardening network devices, offering practical guidance and theoretical insights. Each section dives deeply into strategies for mitigating threats, securing configurations, and enhancing the resilience of these pivotal systems.

The Importance of Hardening Network Devices

The security of network devices is a cornerstone of overall IT security. Vulnerabilities in devices like routers or firewalls can lead to breaches that compromise an organization's entire infrastructure. The critical importance of hardening these devices can be summarized in three key areas:

1. Protecting Network Traffic

Network devices serve as gatekeepers for all communication within an organization. Without proper hardening, attackers can intercept, manipulate, or disrupt this traffic.

Example: A poorly configured router could allow attackers to eavesdrop on sensitive communications, leading to data breaches or unauthorized data access.

2. Mitigating Exploitable Vulnerabilities

Many attacks exploit vulnerabilities in outdated or improperly configured network devices. From denial-of-service attacks to unauthorized remote access, these risks can be minimized with proper hardening.

Case Study: The Mirai botnet exploited vulnerabilities in unsecured IoT devices and routers to launch massive Distributed Denial of Service (DDoS) attacks, crippling websites and online services.

3. Ensuring Compliance

Organizations operating in regulated sectors must secure their network devices to meet compliance standards such as PCI DSS, ISO 27001, and GDPR. Proper hardening helps demonstrate due diligence and avoids costly penalties.

Hardening Routers and Switches

Routers and switches are the backbone of any network, controlling the flow of data between devices. Securing them requires a combination of foundational and advanced measures.

1. Changing Default Credentials

Default usernames and passwords are publicly documented and widely exploited by attackers. Changing these credentials is the first step in securing any network device.

Why It Matters: Attackers often use automated tools to scan for devices with default credentials, gaining unauthorized access within seconds.

Best Practices:

Use strong passwords combining upper and lowercase letters, numbers, and special characters.

Implement regular password changes and avoid reusing old passwords.
Enable Multi-Factor Authentication (MFA) where supported, adding a second layer of verification.

2. Disabling Unnecessary Services

Many routers and switches ship with default services enabled that are not required for operation, such as Telnet or FTP. These services can be exploited to gain access or launch attacks.

Steps to Harden:

Replace Telnet with Secure Shell (SSH) for encrypted remote access.
Disable Simple Network Management Protocol (SNMP) if it is not needed or restrict it to specific trusted hosts.
Deactivate Universal Plug and Play (UPnP), which is often unnecessary in enterprise environments and can be exploited by attackers.
Real-World Application: A misconfigured SNMP service could expose device configurations to attackers, enabling them to manipulate routing tables or disable the device entirely.

3. Implementing Access Control Lists (ACLs)

Access Control Lists (ACLs) act as filters, defining which devices can communicate with the network and under what conditions. They are essential for limiting unauthorized access.

How They Work:

Block traffic from untrusted IP ranges or networks.
Permit only necessary traffic to management interfaces, such as allowing administrative access only from specific IP addresses.
Prevent unauthorized communication between devices on the same network by restricting internal traffic.
Example: By implementing ACLs, an organization can ensure that only specific IP ranges from internal devices can access sensitive systems, reducing the likelihood of unauthorized lateral movement during a breach.

4. Regular Firmware Updates

Firmware is the operating system of a network device. Regular updates are crucial for patching vulnerabilities and adding new security features.

Implementation Guidelines:

Schedule regular checks for firmware updates from device vendors.
Test updates in a controlled environment before deploying them to production devices.
Maintain backups of current configurations before applying updates to allow quick recovery in case of issues.
Historical Insight: The 2017 KRACK attack targeted vulnerabilities in Wi-Fi protocols, which were mitigated through firmware updates released by manufacturers. Many organizations were exposed simply because they failed to update their devices.

Hardening Firewalls

Firewalls are the first line of defense between a private network and external threats. Proper configuration and maintenance of firewalls are critical to ensuring network security.

1. Creating Granular Rules

Firewall rules should operate on the principle of least privilege, allowing only the traffic that is explicitly required and blocking everything else.

Rule Design:

Define specific IP ranges for allowed communication.
Restrict access to sensitive resources to essential personnel only.
Deny all undefined traffic by default to prevent unintended access.
Example: A financial institution might configure its firewall to permit only HTTPS
traffic to its public-facing servers, blocking other protocols to reduce attack
vectors.

2. Implementing Network Segmentation

Segmenting the network into logical zones reduces the potential impact of a breach
by containing attackers within a single segment.

Practical Application:

Separate guest Wi-Fi networks from the corporate LAN.
Use VLANs to isolate sensitive data such as financial records or customer databases
from general employee access.
Security Benefits: In the event of a ransomware attack, segmentation can prevent
the malware from spreading laterally to critical systems.

3. Enabling and Monitoring Logs

Firewall logs are essential for detecting and analyzing suspicious activity.

What to Monitor:

Repeated access attempts from the same external IP.
Attempts to access blocked ports or protocols.
High volumes of traffic from unexpected sources.
Tools: Combine firewall logs with Security Information and Event Management (SIEM)
systems to automate anomaly detection and generate actionable alerts.

Hardening Wireless Access Points

Wireless networks are often targeted by attackers due to their broadcast nature and
ease of access. Proper hardening of access points is critical for maintaining a
secure network.

1. Enforcing Secure Encryption Protocols

Encryption ensures that wireless traffic is protected from eavesdropping and
unauthorized access.

Best Practices:

Use WPA3, the latest Wi-Fi encryption standard, to secure communications.
Disable legacy protocols like WEP and WPA, which are vulnerable to modern attacks.
Case Study: The 2007 TJX breach exploited weaknesses in outdated WEP encryption,
exposing millions of customer records.

2. Hiding SSIDs

Hiding the Service Set Identifier (SSID) can reduce visibility to casual attackers,
making the network less obvious.

Limitations: While this measure deters low-skilled attackers, it does not protect
against determined intruders who can use scanning tools to detect hidden networks.

3. Restricting Access by MAC Address

Whitelisting device MAC addresses limits access to known, authorized devices.

Drawbacks: MAC addresses can be spoofed, so this measure should be combined with
other security controls.

Monitoring and Maintenance

The process of hardening network devices is not static. Continuous monitoring and updates are necessary to maintain security.

1. Conducting Security Audits

Regular audits help identify outdated configurations and emerging vulnerabilities.

Tools:
Nmap for scanning open ports and services.
Nessus for detailed vulnerability assessments.

2. Using Intrusion Detection Systems (IDS)

IDS monitor network traffic for suspicious activity, providing an additional layer of protection.

Capabilities:
Detect brute force attempts on administrative interfaces.
Alert administrators to unusual patterns of traffic or failed login attempts.

3. Maintaining Configuration Backups

Backups allow rapid recovery in case of device failure or malicious tampering.

Best Practices:
Automate regular backups.
Store backups securely offline to prevent tampering.

Conclusion

Hardening network devices is an essential component of a robust security strategy. By combining advanced configurations, regular updates, segmentation, and vigilant monitoring, organizations can protect their networks from evolving threats. This proactive approach secures both individual devices and the entire infrastructure, safeguarding data, and ensuring reliable network operations.

Chapter 9: Hardening Applications – Advanced Security for Critical Software

Introduction

Application software is one of the most vulnerable aspects of IT infrastructure. Applications, whether internal or public-facing, are frequently the targets of cyberattacks due to their direct interaction with users and sensitive data. Misconfigurations or unpatched vulnerabilities can lead to unauthorized access, data breaches, and the compromise of entire systems.

Application hardening involves implementing technical, procedural, and organizational measures to enhance software security. This chapter provides a comprehensive exploration of best practices, advanced tools, and methodologies to secure applications against a broad spectrum of threats. Each section delves into practical strategies and offers detailed examples to guide IT professionals and cybersecurity experts in implementing effective defenses.

The Importance of Application Hardening

Applications serve as the primary interface for users to interact with systems and sensitive data. Their pivotal role necessitates a robust security posture, as even minor oversights can have significant consequences.

Preventing Cyberattacks

Applications often provide the entry point for attackers. Hardening mitigates risks such as unauthorized access, exploitation of vulnerabilities, and data theft.

Detailed Example: A weak login page without rate-limiting allows attackers to perform credential stuffing or brute-force attacks, potentially compromising user accounts. Implementing strong password policies, captchas, and IP-blocking mechanisms significantly reduces this risk.

Protecting Sensitive Data

Applications frequently process and store critical information such as personal details, financial records, and intellectual property. Hardening measures ensure these data sets are safeguarded against unauthorized access and leaks.

Real-World Impact: The 2017 Equifax breach exposed sensitive data of over 147 million individuals due to a failure to patch a known vulnerability in an application framework.

Ensuring Regulatory Compliance

Compliance frameworks like GDPR, HIPAA, and PCI DSS mandate stringent application security practices to protect user data and ensure legal conformity. Failure to adhere can result in heavy fines and reputational damage.

Enhancing Reliability

A secure application is less susceptible to disruptions caused by cyberattacks or system misuse. This improves uptime, user trust, and overall system integrity.

Input Validation

Validating input is a cornerstone of secure application development. Failing to validate input data allows attackers to inject malicious payloads, potentially compromising the entire application.

Sanitization Techniques
Input Whitelisting:

Accept only explicitly allowed data formats. For instance, email fields should strictly adhere to standard patterns like ^[a-zA-Z0-9._%+-]+@[a-zA-Z0-9.-]+\.[a-zA-Z]{2,}$.

Reject all characters or formats that deviate from the defined criteria.

Real-Time Validation:

Implement both client-side and server-side validation. Client-side validation enhances user experience by providing immediate feedback, while server-side validation ensures robust defense against bypass techniques.

Sanitization Libraries:

Utilize industry-standard libraries (e.g., OWASP ESAPI for Java, Django Validation Tools for Python) that offer pre-built sanitization and validation routines.

Advanced Use Case

In an online banking application, where users input account details and amounts fo transactions, strict validation prevents SQL injection or cross-site scripting (XSS). A hardened input validation process would:

Reject unexpected characters such as <> or '.

Log anomalous input attempts for future analysis.

Sanitize inputs by escaping special characters and removing dangerous sequences.

Protecting Against Cross-Site Scripting (XSS)

Cross-Site Scripting (XSS) attacks occur when an application allows users to injec malicious scripts into webpages, enabling attackers to execute these scripts in another user's browser.

Mitigation Strategies
Output Encoding:

Encode all data rendered in the browser to neutralize embedded scripts. For example, replace < with < and > with > to prevent execution.

Content Security Policy (CSP):

Restrict the sources of executable scripts using CSP headers. For instance, a CSP like Content-Security-Policy: script-src 'self' limits script execution to those

hosted by the application itself.
Escaping Dynamic Content:

Use escaping libraries specific to programming languages to ensure dynamic data,
like user comments or profile updates, is safely rendered.
Illustrative Example
In a social networking app, if a user inputs <script>alert('XSS')</script> into
their profile description, the application should encode these tags before
rendering, displaying them as harmless text instead of executing the script.

Session Management Security
Sessions are essential for maintaining user authentication and state in
applications. Poorly secured sessions can lead to session hijacking, fixation, or
impersonation.

Best Practices
Secure Token Generation:

Use cryptographically secure algorithms to generate unique session tokens.
Ensure tokens are large enough to prevent brute-force prediction attacks.
Token Encryption:

Transmit session tokens over HTTPS to prevent interception during transmission.
Expiration Policies:

Implement session expiration to minimize the risk window for hijacking.
Renew tokens periodically during prolonged user activity.
Session Termination:

Ensure tokens are invalidated upon logout and that no residual credentials are
stored on the client-side.
Configuration Hardening
Default configurations often favor usability over security, making them an easy
target for attackers. Reviewing and adjusting these settings is crucial.

Essential Steps
Disable Debug Features:

Disable debugging modes and verbose error messages in production environments.
These often expose sensitive application internals.
Restrict Permissions:

Limit file and resource access strictly to what the application needs.
For instance, restrict write access for configuration files to prevent unauthorized
modifications.
Password Security
Passwords remain a primary authentication mechanism. Strengthening password
management is critical to application security.

Implementation Techniques
Complexity Requirements:

Enforce passwords to include uppercase letters, numbers, and special characters
with a minimum length (e.g., 12 characters).
Secure Storage:

Use modern hashing algorithms like bcrypt or Argon2 to securely store passwords.
Recovery Mechanisms:

Provide secure password reset methods. Instead of sending plain passwords, offer time-limited reset links.

Defending Against Injection Attacks

Injection vulnerabilities, such as SQL injection and command injection, exploit improper handling of input data.

Prevention Methods

Parameterized Queries:

Replace dynamic query construction with parameterized queries or prepared statements.

Minimize Privileges:

Limit database access to essential operations. For example, an application user should not have administrative privileges.

Sanitize Inputs:

Strip harmful characters from input fields to mitigate injection risks.

Conclusion

Application hardening is not a one-time task but a continuous, evolving process. As attackers develop more sophisticated techniques, professionals must proactively implement, test, and refine security measures to stay ahead. By adhering to the strategies detailed in this chapter—ranging from input validation to session management and configuration hardening—organizations can significantly bolster their applications' defenses, ensuring reliability, compliance, and user trust.

Chapter 10: Hardening Network Peripherals – Strengthening the Foundation of Cybersecurity in Detail

Introduction

Network peripherals such as routers, switches, firewalls, and access points form the backbone of any IT infrastructure. These devices are responsible for regulating data flow, safeguarding sensitive resources, and maintaining secure communication between systems. However, their central role also makes them prime targets for cyberattacks. Threat actors exploit misconfigurations, outdated firmware, and unprotected interfaces to compromise networks and access sensitive data.

To mitigate these risks, hardening network peripherals is essential. Hardening refers to the implementation of robust security measures, strict configurations, and ongoing monitoring practices to fortify these devices against threats. This chapter provides an in-depth guide to hardening network peripherals, offering detailed techniques and strategies to help organizations protect their critical infrastructure.

1. Change Default Passwords

Default passwords are among the weakest points in network security. These passwords are often publicly available in device documentation, making it simple for attackers to gain unauthorized access to devices.

Detailed Strategies for Secure Password Management

Understanding Default Risks:

Default credentials, such as "admin" or "password," are the first entry points attackers exploit. These are widely known and are often part of brute force attack dictionaries.

Creating Strong and Unique Passwords:

Use a mix of uppercase letters, lowercase letters, numbers, and symbols.
Ensure passwords are at least 14 characters long to increase resistance to brute force attacks.

Avoid common words, patterns, or easily guessable combinations.
Rotating Passwords Regularly:

Implement policies to change device passwords every 60 to 90 days. Regular changes prevent long-term exploitation in the event of a breach.
Using Password Managers:

Employ password management solutions such as LastPass or KeePass to securely generate, store, and manage passwords. This reduces the risk of credential reuse and manual errors.
Two-Factor Authentication (2FA):

Strengthen device access by enabling 2FA wherever possible, adding an additional layer of security beyond the password.
Practical Example
A corporate firewall retains its default "admin/admin" credentials, which an attacker leverages to reconfigure traffic rules, exposing internal systems to external threats. Changing the credentials to a unique, complex password like "P@ssw0rd2024!Network" and adding 2FA would have mitigated the risk entirely.

2. Disable Unnecessary Services
Default configurations of network devices often include a range of pre-enabled services designed for convenience but unnecessary for most deployments. These services can serve as entry points for attackers.

Best Practices for Service Optimization
Service Audit:

Identify all active services on each network device using diagnostic tools or built-in utilities.
Document these services to establish a baseline and understand their purpose.
Disabling Non-Essential Services:

Turn off insecure protocols like Telnet, FTP, or HTTP. Replace them with secure alternatives such as SSH, SFTP, and HTTPS.
Deactivate legacy management interfaces, especially those accessible over the public internet.
Restricting SNMP Access:

While SNMP (Simple Network Management Protocol) is essential for monitoring, only SNMPv3 should be used. Configure it to accept requests solely from trusted hosts and networks.
Port Control:

Close unnecessary ports to minimize the attack surface. For instance, disable ports associated with unneeded protocols and restrict administrative access to specific IP ranges.
Scenario Example
A router with an open Telnet service is targeted in an attack. By disabling Telnet and enabling SSH with key-based authentication, the risk of credential theft during administrative sessions is eliminated.

3. Regularly Update Firmware and Software
Firmware and software updates address vulnerabilities, enhance functionality, and introduce new security features. However, neglected updates leave devices susceptible to known exploits.

Comprehensive Firmware Update Strategies
Tracking Updates:

Subscribe to vendor advisories and bulletins to stay informed about firmware updates and critical patches.
Testing Updates:

Before deployment, test updates in a sandboxed or non-production environment to verify compatibility with existing configurations.
Automating Updates:

Utilize centralized systems like Cisco DNA Center or Fortinet's FortiManager to automate the update process for multiple devices.
Secure Downloads:

Always download firmware updates directly from manufacturer websites. Validate the files using cryptographic checksums to ensure their integrity.
Backup Before Updating:

Save current configurations to ensure a fallback in case the update causes unforeseen issues.
Real-World Example
The infamous Mirai botnet exploited devices with outdated firmware to launch massive DDoS attacks. Proactive firmware updates would have prevented many of these devices from being compromised.

4. Configure Access Controls and Permissions
Proper access controls are essential to prevent unauthorized changes and ensure accountability in managing network devices.

Implementing Robust Access Controls
Account Separation:

Create individual accounts for each administrator to track actions and enforce accountability.
Role-Based Access Control (RBAC):

Assign permissions based on roles, ensuring that users can access only what they need. For example, a junior admin might only view configurations, while a senior admin has full access.
Network Access Restrictions:

Limit device management access to secure IP ranges using ACLs (Access Control Lists).
Multi-Factor Authentication (MFA):

Enforce MFA to add a layer of verification during login attempts.
Illustrative Case
A network switch configured with shared admin credentials was compromised, leading to unauthorized changes. RBAC and unique credentials would have ensured traceability and minimized the damage.

5. Encrypt All Communications
Encrypted communication prevents attackers from intercepting sensitive data or exploiting unprotected sessions.

Key Practices for Secure Communication
Enable HTTPS:

Replace HTTP with HTTPS for web-based administrative interfaces.
Mandate Secure Shell (SSH):

Use SSH with strong key-based authentication for CLI access instead of Telnet.
Secure SNMP Communications:

Restrict SNMP usage to SNMPv3, which supports encryption and authentication.
TLS Certificates:

Deploy valid TLS certificates for devices to secure administrative portals.
6. Implement Network Segmentation
Network segmentation divides a network into isolated zones, limiting attack
propagation and improving control over sensitive resources.

Segmentation Strategies
Using VLANs:

Create VLANs to separate user groups, sensitive systems, and less secure devices
like IoT.
Firewalls Between Zones:

Deploy firewalls to regulate traffic between segments, ensuring only necessary
communication occurs.
Implementing Zero Trust Policies:

Assume every network zone is potentially compromised. Enforce strict authentication
and validation at every point.
7. Monitor and Log Device Activities
Logging and monitoring provide invaluable insights into potential security
incidents, helping organizations detect and respond promptly.

Key Monitoring Practices
Centralized Log Management:

Collect logs from all devices in a SIEM system like Splunk or Graylog for analysis
and alerting.
Automated Anomaly Detection:

Configure systems to identify and alert administrators about unusual activities,
such as repeated login failures or configuration changes.
8. Regular Configuration Backups
Frequent backups ensure that device settings can be restored quickly in case of a
failure or compromise.

Backup Best Practices
Scheduled Backups:

Automate regular backups using management tools to ensure no configurations are
missed.
Secure Storage:

Encrypt backups and restrict access to them using strong ACLs.
9. Conduct Regular Security Assessments
Security assessments help uncover vulnerabilities and evaluate the effectiveness of
implemented hardening measures.

Penetration Testing and Scans
Vulnerability Scanners:

Use tools like Nessus or OpenVAS to identify weaknesses.
Red Team Simulations:

Simulate sophisticated attack scenarios to test device resilience.
Conclusion
Hardening network peripherals is indispensable in a world where cyber threats are constantly evolving. By implementing comprehensive security measures, updating systems, and monitoring continuously, organizations can significantly reduce risks and protect their infrastructures against advanced attacks.

Chapter 11: Application Hardening – Protecting Software from Vulnerabilities and Threats
Introduction
Modern applications are the operational heart of IT infrastructures, supporting critical processes and enabling seamless interactions between users, systems, and data. However, this complexity and connectivity also make them attractive targets for cyberattacks. Application hardening is a systematic approach to reducing the attack surface, fixing vulnerabilities, and mitigating the risks of compromise.

In this chapter, we will explore advanced techniques for application hardening, addressing common vulnerabilities such as SQL injection and Cross-Site Scripting (XSS), secure session management, and robust data handling. Each section provides detailed theoretical insights and practical steps to make applications more secure and resilient.

1. Rigorous Validation of Input Data
Unvalidated or insufficiently sanitized input data is one of the primary vectors for attacks against applications. Applications often accept input from multiple sources, including users, APIs, files, and databases. Each input represents a potential risk.

Why Input Validation Matters
Key Risks:

Unvalidated inputs can lead to vulnerabilities like SQL injection, XSS, and buffer overflow attacks.
Hackers can exploit these weaknesses to manipulate application logic or gain unauthorized access to data.
Techniques for Validation:

Whitelist Approach: Define strict criteria for acceptable inputs (e.g., a date field should accept only valid date formats).
Regular Expressions: Use regex to ensure inputs like email addresses and phone numbers conform to expected patterns.
Length Validation: Restrict input size to avoid buffer overflows and performance issues.
Practical Example:

A registration form's "email" field should validate inputs against a regex pattern such as:
less
Copy code
```
^[a-zA-Z0-9._%+-]+@[a-zA-Z0-9.-]+\.[a-zA-Z]{2,}$
```
Invalid data should be rejected with clear, user-friendly error messages.
Advanced Validations:

For API inputs, validate payloads against schemas (e.g., using JSON Schema for RES APIs).
Use libraries such as Joi (for Node.js) or Validator.js to standardize and simplif validation.
2. Protection Against Injection Attacks

Injection attacks, such as SQL injection, are among the most dangerous threats to applications. These attacks exploit improperly sanitized inputs to insert malicious commands that alter the application's behavior.

Defensive Measures Against Injection Attacks
Parameterized Queries and Prepared Statements:

Always use parameterized queries to separate SQL logic from user input. For example:
sql
Copy code
```sql
SELECT * FROM users WHERE email = ? AND password = ?;
```
This ensures user input is treated strictly as data, not executable code.
Sanitization of Inputs:

Escape special characters like ', ", and -- to neutralize malicious payloads.
Use sanitization libraries tailored for the application's language or framework.
Object-Relational Mapping (ORM):

ORMs such as Hibernate or SQLAlchemy abstract database interactions, minimizing direct exposure to SQL.
Database-Level Protections:

Limit database privileges to prevent unauthorized access. For instance, the application should connect with a user account that has only SELECT permissions for sensitive queries.
3. Secure Session Management
Sessions allow applications to maintain user state during interactions. Poorly managed sessions can expose vulnerabilities such as session hijacking and fixation.

Best Practices for Session Management
Secure Token Generation:

Use cryptographically secure random functions to generate session tokens.
Ensure tokens are unique and unpredictable.
Implementing HTTPOnly and Secure Flags:

Use the HTTPOnly flag to prevent JavaScript access to cookies, mitigating XSS risks.
Set the Secure flag to ensure cookies are transmitted only over HTTPS.
Session Expiration and Renewal:

Set idle timeouts to terminate inactive sessions.
Refresh tokens periodically to prevent fixation attacks.
Token Storage and Transmission:

Store session tokens in secure, encrypted storage (e.g., HTTP cookies or secure storage in mobile apps).
4. Enforce HTTPS Across All Communications
HTTPS is essential for securing data exchanges between clients and servers. It ensures confidentiality, integrity, and authenticity of transmitted data.

Steps to Secure HTTPS Implementation
TLS Versions:

Avoid outdated protocols like SSLv3 or TLS 1.0. Use TLS 1.2 or TLS 1.3.
Certificate Management:

Obtain SSL/TLS certificates from trusted Certificate Authorities (CAs).

Rotate and renew certificates before expiration.
HTTP Strict Transport Security (HSTS):

Configure HSTS headers to enforce HTTPS and prevent protocol downgrade attacks:
lua
Copy code
Strict-Transport-Security: max-age=31536000; includeSubDomains; preload
Regular Scans:

Use tools like SSL Labs to test and validate HTTPS configurations.
5. Continuous Monitoring and Logging
Monitoring application activity is critical for detecting threats, understanding usage patterns, and responding to incidents.

Effective Logging Strategies
Granular Event Logging:

Log critical events such as:
Failed login attempts.
Privilege escalations.
Access from unknown IPs or devices.
Log Protection:

Encrypt logs to prevent tampering.
Store logs in centralized, secure locations accessible only to authorized personnel.
Analysis and Alerting:

Use SIEM tools like Splunk or ELK Stack to aggregate and analyze logs for anomalies.
6. XSS Prevention
Cross-Site Scripting (XSS) enables attackers to inject malicious scripts into web pages viewed by users, potentially compromising sensitive data.

Techniques for XSS Mitigation
Input Sanitization:

Sanitize and escape all user inputs displayed in the browser.
Use libraries like OWASP's ESAPI to ensure comprehensive sanitization.
Content Security Policy (CSP):

Define CSP headers to restrict the execution of scripts to trusted sources:
css
Copy code
Content-Security-Policy: default-src 'self';
Escaping Outputs:

Encode HTML and JavaScript outputs to neutralize injected scripts.
7. Data Backups and Recovery
Regular backups are essential to safeguard against data corruption, loss, or ransomware attacks.

Robust Backup Strategies
Automation:

Schedule automatic backups to secure storage systems (e.g., cloud storage or dedicated backup servers).
Testing:

Conduct periodic restoration tests to verify data integrity and accessibility.
Encryption:

Encrypt backups to prevent unauthorized access.

8. Principle of Least Privilege (PoLP)

Limiting access rights to only what is necessary reduces the risk of insider threats and unauthorized actions.

Implementation of PoLP
Role-Based Access Control (RBAC):

Define roles with minimal permissions.
Regularly review and adjust access levels.
Service Accounts:

Assign separate, limited-access accounts for application components and automated scripts.

9. Security Testing

Regular testing uncovers vulnerabilities and strengthens application defenses.

Types of Security Testing
Penetration Testing:

Simulate real-world attacks to identify weaknesses.
Static Code Analysis:

Use tools like SonarQube to detect insecure coding practices.
Dynamic Testing:

Employ tools like OWASP ZAP to identify runtime vulnerabilities.

Conclusion

Application hardening is an essential, ongoing effort to protect software from evolving threats. Through rigorous input validation, secure session management, robust data handling, and continuous testing, organizations can significantly mitigate risks. A hardened application not only protects sensitive data but also ensures trust and reliability for its users.

Chapter 12: Hardening Network Devices – Comprehensive Protection Against External and Internal Threats

Introduction

Network devices such as routers, switches, firewalls, and access points are the backbone of modern IT infrastructures. These devices control the flow of data, ensure connectivity, and serve as the first line of defense against cyber threats. Their central role makes them prime targets for attackers aiming to compromise networks, steal data, or disrupt operations. Weak configurations, outdated firmware, or neglected security measures can result in severe vulnerabilities.

Hardening network devices is the systematic process of securing them by applying robust configurations, enabling advanced security features, and continuously monitoring for anomalies. This chapter provides an exhaustive exploration of network device hardening techniques, highlighting practical methods, common vulnerabilities, and strategies to mitigate risks effectively.

1. Changing Default Passwords

Default passwords are among the easiest vulnerabilities to exploit in network devices. Manufacturers often ship devices with preset credentials, such as admin/admin or root/password. These credentials are publicly documented, making it trivial for attackers to use them in brute-force or automated attacks.

Why Change Default Passwords?
Elimination of Publicly Known Weaknesses:

Default passwords are often the first target of cyberattacks, especially during
reconnaissance or large-scale botnet attacks.
Best Practices for Secure Passwords:

Use complex passwords: At least 12-16 characters combining uppercase, lowercase,
numbers, and special symbols.
Implement a regular rotation policy to change passwords periodically.
Avoid using easily guessable patterns, such as company names or device serial
numbers.
Practical Implementation:

After initial setup, configure unique passwords for each device. For example, an
enterprise router should use credentials like 3xTr@_RouTr2024! instead of
admin/admin.
Enhancing Security with MFA:

Multi-Factor Authentication (MFA) adds an extra layer of protection by requiring an
additional verification factor, such as a one-time password sent to a mobile
device.
2. Disabling Unnecessary Services
Network devices often come with pre-enabled services that may not be necessary for
their intended use. These services can introduce vulnerabilities if left unchecked.

Steps to Minimize Attack Surface
Identify Active Services:

Audit the services enabled on each device using management interfaces or command-
line tools.
Common services to review include Telnet, HTTP, SNMP, and FTP.
Disable Insecure or Redundant Services:

Replace Telnet with SSH for secure remote access.
Use HTTPS instead of HTTP for management interfaces.
Configure SNMPv3 for secure network monitoring or disable SNMP entirely if
unnecessary.
Practical Example:

A switch configured with Telnet should disable it (no telnet in CLI commands) and
enable SSH for encrypted management traffic.
Document and Verify Changes:

Maintain a log of disabled services and validate configurations through periodic
audits.
3. Regular Firmware and Software Updates
Firmware and software updates address vulnerabilities, improve functionality, and
enhance security. Neglecting updates exposes devices to exploitation by attackers
leveraging known weaknesses.

Implementing an Update Policy
Regular Version Checks:

Use a schedule to check for updates on the manufacturer's website or through
automated management tools.
Testing Before Deployment:

Apply updates in a test environment to verify compatibility with existing

configurations and applications.
Secure Downloads:

Obtain firmware only from trusted sources, ensuring it is free from tampering by verifying digital signatures.
Backup Configuration Pre-Update:

Always back up current configurations before applying updates to enable quick recovery if needed.
Practical Example:

A firewall updated with the latest firmware patches can mitigate critical exploits like the VPNFilter vulnerability.
4. Configuring Access Control Lists (ACLs)
Access Control Lists are critical tools for managing and filtering network traffic. Properly configured ACLs can restrict unauthorized access and improve the overall security posture.

Effective ACL Implementation
Limit Management Access:

Restrict administrative access to known and trusted IP addresses. For example:
makefile
Copy code
Permit: 10.0.1.0/24 (Management VLAN)
Deny: All Others
Control Traffic Between Subnets:

Prevent lateral movement within the network by blocking unnecessary inter-VLAN communication.
Restrict Inbound Traffic:

Deny traffic to critical ports (e.g., 23 for Telnet, 3389 for RDP) unless explicitly required.
Audit and Refine Rules Regularly:

Periodically review ACL configurations to ensure they align with current network requirements.
5. Encrypting Remote Management Communications
Remote management often involves the transmission of sensitive credentials and commands. Unencrypted protocols can expose this information to attackers through packet sniffing or man-in-the-middle attacks.

Key Steps for Securing Management Traffic
Enable Encrypted Protocols:

Use SSH instead of Telnet for CLI access.
Configure HTTPS for GUI-based interfaces with valid SSL/TLS certificates.
Configure Certificate Management:

Regularly renew and replace SSL/TLS certificates to prevent their expiration or compromise.
Practical Example:

Disabling HTTP and enabling HTTPS with a self-signed or CA-issued certificate on a router's management interface ensures secure communication.
6. Network Segmentation
Network segmentation reduces the risk of widespread compromise by isolating sensitive systems and controlling inter-segment traffic.

How to Segment Effectively
Define VLANs for Logical Separation:

Separate traffic based on function (e.g., user devices, IoT, servers).
Firewall Enforcement:

Implement firewalls between VLANs to control and inspect inter-segment
communication.
Example Use Case:

Isolate IoT devices in a separate VLAN with restricted access to corporate
networks, mitigating risks posed by potentially insecure devices.
7. Monitoring and Logging
Comprehensive monitoring is crucial for detecting and responding to suspicious
activity on network devices.

Best Practices for Effective Monitoring
Centralized Log Aggregation:

Send logs to a Security Information and Event Management (SIEM) system for real-
time analysis and long-term storage.
Monitor Key Events:

Focus on login attempts, configuration changes, and traffic anomalies.
Automated Alerts:

Set up alerts for critical events, such as repeated login failures or unauthorize
access attempts.
8. Regular Configuration Backups
Backing up configurations ensures that devices can be quickly restored to their
last known good state following failures or attacks.

Backup Strategies
Automate Backups:

Schedule backups using centralized tools or device features.
Secure Storage:

Encrypt backup files and store them in access-restricted locations.
Test Restore Procedures:

Regularly verify the ability to restore backups to ensure reliability.
9. Implementing Two-Factor Authentication (2FA)
Two-Factor Authentication strengthens login security by requiring a second
verification method.

Deploying 2FA
Token-Based Systems:

Use apps like Google Authenticator to generate time-based one-time passwords
(TOTP).
Hardware Keys:

Integrate USB security tokens (e.g., YubiKey) for physical authentication.
Practical Example:

Enable 2FA for admin accounts on a firewall, requiring both a password and a TOTP
for login.

10. Penetration Testing and Security Audits

Regularly testing network devices through penetration testing helps uncover hidden vulnerabilities.

Conducting Penetration Tests
Simulate Real-World Attacks:

Use tools like Nmap, Nessus, or Metasploit to identify weaknesses.
Fix Identified Vulnerabilities:

Apply patches, reconfigure settings, and refine ACLs based on test results.
Repeat Regularly:

Schedule tests quarterly or after significant network changes.
Conclusion
Hardening network devices is a cornerstone of modern cybersecurity, requiring meticulous planning and execution. By changing default passwords, disabling unnecessary services, enabling encryption, and implementing robust monitoring, organizations can significantly enhance the resilience of their infrastructure. Combining proactive updates, segmented networks, and regular testing ensures a layered defense against both external and internal threats. As networks grow increasingly complex, these practices remain essential for safeguarding critical assets and maintaining operational integrity.

Chapter 13: Hardening Applications – Fortifying Software Against Vulnerabilities and Attacks

Introduction
Applications are the operational backbone of modern IT infrastructures, driving business processes, managing sensitive data, and enabling connectivity between users and systems. However, their complexity and extensive interconnectivity make them a prime target for cyberattacks. Application hardening is the deliberate process of enhancing application security by reducing vulnerabilities, enforcing strict configurations, and implementing preventive measures to mitigate risks.

This chapter dives into advanced strategies for application hardening, covering protection against vulnerabilities, ensuring secure configurations, and mitigating exploit risks. Each section is expanded with detailed explanations, practical examples, and professional insights to provide a comprehensive guide for cybersecurity practitioners.

1. Protecting Against Known Vulnerabilities

Addressing known vulnerabilities is the cornerstone of application hardening. Publicly documented vulnerabilities, often cataloged in Common Vulnerabilities and Exposures (CVEs), are frequently exploited by attackers. A notable example is CVE-2021-44228 (Log4Shell), which demonstrated how a single, overlooked vulnerability could lead to widespread exploitation.

Strategies for Addressing Known Vulnerabilities:
Establish a Patch Management Process:

Implement an automated patch management system to identify and apply patches promptly.
Prioritize critical updates based on the severity and exploitability of vulnerabilities, using tools like the CVSS (Common Vulnerability Scoring System) for assessment.
Regular Vulnerability Scanning:

Use tools like Nessus, Qualys, or OpenVAS to scan applications and infrastructure regularly.

Cross-reference scan results with CVE databases to identify urgent vulnerabilities.
Continuous Monitoring and Notifications:

Subscribe to security advisory feeds from vendors and organizations like NIST or
MITRE.
Integrate tools like Dependabot or Snyk into development pipelines to flag
vulnerable dependencies in real-time.
Secure Deployment Pipelines:

Use DevSecOps practices to ensure all builds are tested for vulnerabilities before
deployment.
Include security gates that block deployment if critical vulnerabilities are
detected.
2. Input Validation
Many successful attacks exploit insufficient input validation, injecting malicious
data to manipulate application behavior. Robust input validation is critical to
maintaining application integrity and preventing exploitation.

Best Practices for Input Validation:
Adopt a Whitelist Approach:

Allow only specific, pre-approved data formats. For example, a date field should
accept only valid date strings (e.g., "YYYY-MM-DD").
Apply Contextual Encoding:

Encode data based on where it is used. For example, encode user-generated content
for HTML contexts to prevent XSS attacks.
Reject Unexpected Data Early:

Use server-side validation to supplement client-side checks, as client-side
validation alone can be bypassed by attackers.
Limit Input Length:

Define maximum lengths for all input fields. For instance, usernames might have a
maximum of 30 characters.
Practical Example:

```python
Copy code
import re

def validate_username(username):
    pattern = r'^[a-zA-Z0-9_.-]{3,30}$'
    if not re.match(pattern, username):
        raise ValueError("Invalid username format")
```
3. Defending Against Injection Attacks
Injection attacks, such as SQL injection, command injection, and LDAP injection,
occur when untrusted inputs manipulate application queries or commands.

Comprehensive Countermeasures for Injection Attacks:
Parameterized Queries:

Use prepared statements or parameterized queries to separate commands from data.
This prevents malicious inputs from altering query structures.
```sql
Copy code
SELECT * FROM users WHERE username = ? AND password = ?
```
Stored Procedures:

Enforce database operations through predefined procedures, limiting direct query execution.
Sanitize Inputs:

Escape special characters in user inputs to prevent command or query manipulation.
Input Validation Frameworks:

Use libraries like OWASP ESAPI to enforce strong input validation.
Database Hardening:

Grant applications minimal database privileges and restrict the use of potentially dangerous functions like xp_cmdshell in SQL Server.
4. Secure Session Management
Improper session handling is a major vector for attacks such as session hijacking, fixation, and replay attacks. Robust session management safeguards user interactions and application integrity.

Techniques for Secure Session Management:
Generate Secure Tokens:

Tokens must be unique, unpredictable, and use sufficient entropy. Implement cryptographically secure random generators.
Session Timeouts:

Set idle session timeouts to prevent unauthorized reuse. For example, log out users after 15 minutes of inactivity.
Restrict Cookie Access:

Use the HttpOnly and Secure flags in cookies to prevent access via JavaScript and enforce HTTPS transmission.
Token Binding:

Bind session tokens to client properties, such as IP address and browser fingerprint, to detect anomalies.
Revalidate Tokens:

Require token regeneration upon privilege changes or sensitive operations.
5. Implementing HTTPS and Strong Encryption
Encryption ensures that sensitive data remains confidential, even if intercepted.

Key Encryption Practices:
Force HTTPS:

Redirect all HTTP traffic to HTTPS and implement HSTS headers to enforce secure connections.
TLS Configuration:

Disable outdated protocols (e.g., TLS 1.0/1.1) and enable modern cryptographic suites like TLS 1.3.
Encrypt Data at Rest:

Use AES-256 for encrypting sensitive data stored in databases or file systems.
Certificate Management:

Regularly renew SSL/TLS certificates and use wildcard or multi-domain certificates where applicable.
6. Access Control and Authorization
Restricting access ensures users and services only perform authorized actions.

Advanced Access Control Techniques:
Role-Based Access Control (RBAC):

Assign permissions based on predefined roles, such as "Admin" or "Editor."
Attribute-Based Access Control (ABAC):

Incorporate user attributes, such as department or location, to refine access
decisions.
Enforce Policy Checks:

Validate permissions at every request to prevent unauthorized access due to
insecure direct object references (IDOR).
Privileged Access Management (PAM):

Regularly audit and restrict access to high-privilege accounts.
7. Monitoring, Logging, and Threat Detection
Constant monitoring is critical for identifying potential attacks in real-time.

Logging and Monitoring Best Practices:
Capture Detailed Logs:

Record login attempts, failed authentications, and configuration changes.
Centralize Logs:

Use SIEM tools like Splunk or ELK Stack to aggregate and analyze logs across
systems.
Set Alert Thresholds:

Define triggers for suspicious activity, such as multiple failed login attempts.
8. Regular Testing and Validation
Testing validates that applications adhere to security standards and are free from
vulnerabilities.

Testing Approaches:
Dynamic Application Security Testing (DAST):

Simulate runtime attacks to detect issues like XSS and SQL injection.
Static Application Security Testing (SAST):

Analyze source code for vulnerabilities during development.
Penetration Testing:

Conduct comprehensive security assessments simulating real-world attack scenarios.
Automated Scanning:

Integrate tools like OWASP ZAP into CI/CD pipelines for continuous vulnerability
assessments.
Conclusion
Application hardening is a multi-faceted and ongoing effort that combines secure
development practices, vigilant monitoring, and proactive vulnerability management.
By adopting the robust strategies outlined in this chapter, organizations can
significantly enhance their applications' security posture, ensuring resilience
against an ever-evolving landscape of cyber threats.

Chapter 14: Monitoring and Logging – Surveillance and Comprehensive System Analysis
Introduction
Monitoring and logging are indispensable components of any secure and reliable IT
environment. Monitoring involves real-time tracking of system activities,
resources, and behaviors, while logging focuses on the detailed recording of events

or retrospective analysis. Together, these practices form a cornerstone of cybersecurity, enabling organizations to detect anomalies, respond to threats, and optimize system performance effectively.

This chapter explores advanced techniques for monitoring and logging, delving into practical applications, sophisticated tools, and strategies to implement robust surveillance systems. It also discusses how these methodologies integrate seamlessly into DevOps workflows and cloud environments, ensuring modern infrastructures remain secure and efficient.

The Importance of Monitoring and Logging
Monitoring and logging go beyond routine operational tasks to become strategic tools for maintaining security and ensuring operational efficiency. Without these frameworks, organizations are left vulnerable to attacks, inefficiencies, and compliance risks.

Key Benefits
Attack Prevention: Real-time monitoring of network traffic and system activities helps identify unauthorized access attempts or suspicious behavior, enabling proactive defense measures.

Vulnerability Detection: Analyzing logs allows organizations to spot recurring patterns that indicate potential vulnerabilities, such as frequent failed login attempts or unusual access requests.

Incident Forensics: Detailed logs serve as a chronological account of events, aiding investigators in pinpointing the root causes of security breaches and crafting targeted countermeasures.

Performance Optimization: Monitoring identifies bottlenecks and inefficiencies, allowing IT teams to allocate resources better and improve overall system performance.

Regulatory Compliance: Many security standards, including GDPR, HIPAA, and PCI DSS, mandate robust logging practices and the secure retention of log data to ensure transparency and accountability.

Implementing System Monitoring
Monitoring a system effectively involves tracking various components such as hardware resources, processes, network traffic, and application behavior. Each aspect demands specialized tools and configurations for accurate and actionable insights.

1. Monitoring Hardware Resources
Hardware is the foundation of any IT infrastructure, and its health directly impacts system stability. Metrics such as CPU utilization, memory consumption, disk performance, and component temperatures must be monitored to preempt potential failures.

Advanced Practices:

Tools like Nagios or Zabbix allow administrators to set threshold-based alerts. For instance, a server with consistently high CPU usage could indicate a malware infection or a misconfigured application.
Implement predictive analytics to forecast hardware failures by analyzing long-term trends in resource utilization and wear-and-tear.
2. Monitoring Processes and Services
Tracking the processes and services running on a system is critical for identifying unauthorized or malicious activities. Processes that consume excessive resources or

establish unexpected external connections often signal a compromise.

Tools and Techniques:

Use Prometheus and Grafana to create interactive dashboards that display real-time data about process activity, including resource usage and network interactions. Set up automatic alerts for anomalous process behavior, such as sudden spikes in memory usage or processes initiating unexpected network traffic.
3. Monitoring Network Traffic
The network is a primary target for attackers, making traffic analysis essential. Monitoring network activity helps identify signs of malicious actions, including port scans, DDoS attacks, and unauthorized data exfiltration.

Techniques:

Deploy network packet analyzers like Wireshark to capture and inspect traffic at the packet level.
Implement Intrusion Detection Systems (IDS) like Snort or Zeek to automatically flag suspicious traffic patterns, such as repetitive requests to sensitive endpoints or high volumes of data leaving the network.
Creating Detailed Logs
Logs serve as the foundational records for understanding system behavior. For logs to be effective, they must be detailed, well-structured, and easy to analyze.

What to Log
Comprehensive logging ensures that all critical activities are recorded without overburdening the system with unnecessary data. Key events to log include:

Authentication Events: Record all login attempts, including successful and failed attempts, with timestamps, source IPs, and user details.

Configuration Changes: Log any alterations to system settings, application configurations, or network policies to ensure traceability.

Access to Sensitive Data: Monitor who accessed or modified critical data, includin timestamps and user roles.

System Errors and Failures: Capture details of crashes, errors, and exceptions to aid in troubleshooting and debugging.

Log Structuring
Using a standardized format like JSON or XML ensures logs are consistent and can b processed by automated tools.

Example of JSON Log:

json
Copy code
```json
{
  "timestamp": "2024-12-05T10:00:00Z",
  "event": "authentication_attempt",
  "username": "admin",
  "status": "failed",
  "source_ip": "192.168.10.15"
}
```
Centralized Logging Systems
Centralized logging consolidates data from multiple systems, making it easier to analyze and correlate events. Platforms like ELK Stack (Elasticsearch, Logstash, Kibana) or Graylog provide powerful search and visualization tools, enabling faste

detection of issues.

Automated Log Analysis
Modern infrastructures benefit from AI-driven log analysis tools that can detect
patterns and anomalies beyond human capabilities. Machine learning models can
identify hidden trends, such as subtle increases in failed login attempts that may
signal a coordinated attack.

Integrating Monitoring and Logging into DevOps
In a DevOps environment, monitoring and logging must be deeply integrated into
Continuous Integration/Continuous Deployment (CI/CD) workflows. This ensures that
any issues introduced by new code releases or system changes are promptly
identified and resolved.

Strategies for Integration:
Use Prometheus for monitoring application performance during and after deployment.
Implement Fluentd for logging in CI/CD pipelines, ensuring consistent log
collection and analysis.
Automate anomaly detection during deployments, allowing rapid rollback if issues
are detected.
Advanced Best Practices
1. Log Retention Policies
Define clear policies for retaining logs based on organizational needs and
regulatory requirements. For instance, GDPR mandates specific retention periods for
logs containing personal data.

2. Sensitive Log Handling
Segregate logs containing sensitive information, such as personal data or financial
details, and encrypt them to prevent unauthorized access.

3. Proactive Threat Detection
Leverage AI and machine learning for predictive analytics. These tools can flag
potential issues before they escalate into full-blown incidents.

4. Incident Simulations
Regularly simulate security incidents to test the efficacy of your monitoring and
logging systems. Validate that logs capture the necessary details for forensic
analysis and troubleshooting.

Conclusion
Monitoring and logging are vital for maintaining a secure and resilient IT
environment. They enable organizations to detect threats, optimize performance, and
meet compliance requirements. By adopting advanced tools, integrating these
practices into workflows, and leveraging automation, IT teams can ensure their
systems remain robust against the ever-evolving landscape of cyber threats. With
proactive strategies and continuous improvement, monitoring and logging become not
just operational necessities but strategic assets in safeguarding modern
infrastructures.

Chapter 15: Advanced Techniques for Application Hardening
Introduction
The hardening of applications is an essential pillar of modern cybersecurity,
providing robust defenses against a wide array of threats and vulnerabilities.
Applications serve as the interface between users, systems, and critical data,
making them attractive targets for attackers. As the IT landscape evolves with
distributed architectures, DevOps practices, and microservices, application
hardening has become increasingly complex and vital.

This chapter delves into advanced strategies for application hardening, offering comprehensive insights into both theoretical and practical approaches. Each technique is designed to address specific risks, mitigate vulnerabilities, and ensure resilience against sophisticated attacks.

1. Validation and Sanitization of Input Data
Comprehensive Input Validation
Input validation is the foundation of secure application design. Any data entering an application—whether from users, APIs, or external systems—must be scrutinized to ensure it meets strict criteria. Failure to validate inputs can lead to exploitation through attacks like SQL injection, command injection, and cross-site scripting (XSS).

Key Techniques
Data Format Validation: Employ regular expressions to ensure inputs adhere to expected formats. For instance, validating email addresses or phone numbers with precise regex patterns:
regex
Copy code
^[a-zA-Z0-9._%+-]+@[a-zA-Z0-9.-]+\.[a-zA-Z]{2,}$
Type Enforcement: Ensure inputs conform to expected data types. For example, numeric fields should reject alphabetic or special characters.
Length Constraints: Restrict input length to prevent buffer overflows or resource exhaustion attacks.
Real-World Application
For a login form, input fields should be validated to ensure that:

The username contains only alphanumeric characters and underscores.
The password meets complexity requirements, such as including uppercase letters, numbers, and special symbols.
Thorough Input Sanitization
Sanitization focuses on neutralizing potentially dangerous input by escaping or removing malicious characters. This step is crucial for rendering user-generated content safely in web applications.

Practical Approaches
Escape HTML special characters like <, >, &, and ' to prevent their interpretation as code.
Use trusted libraries like OWASP Java Encoder for efficient sanitization across programming languages.
2. Defense Against Injection Attacks
Injection attacks remain among the most prevalent and damaging exploits in application security. They occur when attackers manipulate inputs to execute unintended commands, gain unauthorized access, or retrieve sensitive data.

Parameterized Queries
Parameterized queries are a cornerstone defense against SQL injection. By segregating command syntax from data inputs, they prevent malicious payloads from altering the intended query structure.

Example in Python with SQLite
python
Copy code
cursor.execute("SELECT * FROM users WHERE username = ?", (username,))
Object-Relational Mapping (ORM)
ORM frameworks, such as Hibernate (Java) and SQLAlchemy (Python), abstract database interactions, inherently protecting against common injection vulnerabilities.

Advantages
Automatic query sanitization.

Reduced developer reliance on manual SQL query construction.
Additional Techniques
Input Whitelisting: Restrict input to predefined values, such as fixed dropdown options.
Stored Procedures: Encapsulate database logic to limit dynamic query execution.
3. Secure Session Management
Session management is critical for maintaining user authentication and authorization. However, insecure practices can lead to session hijacking, fixation, or replay attacks.

Advanced Session Practices
Secure Token Generation: Generate session tokens using cryptographically secure random functions. Tokens should be unique, unpredictable, and long enough to resist brute-force attacks.

Anti-CSRF Measures: Include anti-CSRF tokens in all forms to validate the legitimacy of requests, ensuring they originate from the correct user session.

Session Timeout: Automatically expire inactive sessions after a predefined duration, such as 15 minutes. This minimizes the risk of compromised sessions remaining active.

Session Binding: Associate session tokens with specific client attributes, such as IP addresses or user agents, to prevent reuse in unauthorized contexts.

Simultaneous Session Restriction: Limit users to one active session at a time, invalidating previous sessions upon new logins.

4. Advanced Encryption Techniques
Encryption ensures the confidentiality and integrity of sensitive data, whether at rest or in transit.

Transport Encryption
Implement TLS 1.3 for all communication channels to secure data exchanges between clients and servers. Older protocols like TLS 1.0 or SSL must be disabled to eliminate known vulnerabilities.

Example
Use strong ciphers and enforce HTTP Strict Transport Security (HSTS) headers:

http
Copy code
Strict-Transport-Security: max-age=31536000; includeSubDomains; preload
Encryption at Rest
For stored sensitive data, such as passwords or credit card numbers:

Use bcrypt or Argon2 for hashing passwords.
Encrypt databases with AES-256, ensuring keys are stored securely using solutions like AWS Key Management Service (KMS).
5. Implementation of Zero Trust Models
The Zero Trust model fundamentally transforms application security by eliminating implicit trust. Every access request must be verified, regardless of its origin.

Core Principles
Dynamic Authentication: Continuously validate user identity through multi-factor authentication (MFA) and context-aware checks.
Micro-Segmentation: Divide applications into isolated components to limit the scope of potential breaches.
Least Privilege Access: Grant users and processes only the permissions necessary to

perform their roles.
6. Protection Against XSS Attacks
Cross-site scripting (XSS) allows attackers to execute malicious scripts in users' browsers, often leading to data theft or session hijacking.

Preventative Measures
Output Encoding: Encode all user-generated content before rendering it in a web page. For instance, use HTML entity encoding to neutralize tags like <script>.
Content Security Policies (CSP): Define strict rules for script execution:
http
Copy code
Content-Security-Policy: script-src 'self' https://trusted-cdn.com
7. Tools for Application Hardening
A robust application security strategy leverages advanced tools for vulnerability detection and mitigation.

Essential Tools
Burp Suite: Comprehensive platform for penetration testing and vulnerability analysis.
OWASP ZAP: Open-source scanner for identifying common application weaknesses.
SonarQube: Performs Static Application Security Testing (SAST) to detect code vulnerabilities.
Acunetix: Dynamic Application Security Testing (DAST) tool for runtime vulnerability analysis.
8. Monitoring and Logging
Monitoring and logging provide critical insights into application behavior, aiding in anomaly detection and incident response.

Best Practices
Log Key Events: Record all user authentication attempts, privilege changes, and access to sensitive data.
Centralized Logging: Aggregate logs in platforms like ELK Stack for efficient analysis and visualization.
Real-Time Alerts: Configure alerts for suspicious activities, such as repeated failed login attempts or unauthorized configuration changes.
Conclusion
Advanced application hardening is a multi-faceted process requiring meticulous implementation of security best practices, from input validation to session management and encryption. By integrating robust monitoring, leveraging specialized tools, and adopting a proactive Zero Trust framework, organizations can significantly enhance application resilience against evolving threats. These comprehensive strategies ensure the secure and reliable operation of applications in dynamic IT environments.

Chapter 16: Detection and Mitigation of Advanced Attacks
Introduction
Advanced cyberattacks are characterized by their sophistication, persistence, and ability to evade traditional security measures. These include Advanced Persistent Threats (APTs), advanced ransomware variants, and zero-day exploits. To defend against such threats, organizations must adopt proactive detection and robust mitigation strategies that integrate state-of-the-art tools, behavioral analysis, and incident response frameworks. This chapter provides a detailed exploration of advanced techniques to identify, analyze, and neutralize such sophisticated threats, offering professionals practical insights and methodologies.

1. Recognizing Attack Indicators
The first line of defense against advanced attacks is the ability to recognize subtle signs that indicate a breach or attempted intrusion. While traditional security systems may miss these indicators, a trained eye and advanced tools can

identify them before significant damage occurs.

Key Indicators of Advanced Threats
Network Traffic Anomalies: A sudden increase in outbound traffic, unusual connections to external servers, or unexpected activity on non-standard ports may indicate data exfiltration or communication with command-and-control (C2) servers. For instance, a workstation communicating with an external IP flagged in a threat intelligence database is a red flag.

File Integrity Changes: Unexplained modifications to system files, configuration settings, or the appearance of suspicious executables suggest potential malware deployment or unauthorized access.

Unusual Account Activity: Indicators include multiple failed login attempts, access to resources outside regular working hours, or the escalation of privileges for accounts without justification.

Implementation of Advanced Monitoring
Deploying tools such as Security Information and Event Management (SIEM) platforms—Splunk, LogRhythm, or QRadar—enables centralized monitoring and correlation of these indicators, providing real-time alerts and actionable insights.

2. Behavioral Analysis Techniques
Behavioral analysis is a powerful method for identifying threats that evade signature-based detection. It relies on understanding what constitutes "normal" behavior for users, devices, and applications, and flags deviations that could signify an attack.

How Behavioral Analysis Works
Machine Learning Algorithms: Advanced algorithms analyze historical data to establish baselines for normal activity. For example, an algorithm might flag a server that begins communicating with an unknown IP at a high frequency, as this deviates from its regular behavior.

Anomaly Detection Models: These models compare current activity against baselines. For instance, if a user with administrative privileges accesses sensitive files from a new geographic location, the system flags this as unusual.

Practical Applications
Insider Threat Detection: Identify employees accessing data outside their job scope.
Suspicious Process Analysis: Detect processes that attempt to hide or execute payloads in an unusual manner.
Behavioral analysis tools like Exabeam or Vectra AI are increasingly essential in detecting and responding to advanced threats.

3. Mitigating Threats in Real-Time
Rapid mitigation is critical to minimize the damage caused by advanced attacks. Real-time responses rely on predefined policies, automated tools, and human intervention.

Real-Time Isolation
When a device exhibits behavior indicative of compromise, isolating it from the network prevents lateral movement. For instance:

EDR Systems: Endpoint Detection and Response tools, such as CrowdStrike or SentinelOne, can automatically quarantine a device while retaining logs for forensic analysis.
Automated Policy Enforcement

Organizations can predefine policies that trigger mitigation actions based on detected threats. For example:

Blocking IP addresses associated with C2 servers.
Restricting access to critical systems during a detected intrusion.
Automating these actions reduces response times, often neutralizing threats before they escalate.

4. Leveraging Advanced Detection Tools
Advanced attacks require sophisticated tools capable of identifying and analyzing complex threats. Organizations must deploy a suite of technologies to ensure comprehensive visibility.

Intrusion Detection and Prevention Systems (IDS/IPS)
IDS/IPS systems are designed to monitor network traffic, detect malicious activity and, in the case of IPS, actively block it. Popular options include:

Snort: An open-source IDS that provides real-time analysis and alerting.
Suricata: A versatile IDS/IPS with integrated threat detection capabilities.
Threat Intelligence Platforms
Threat intelligence platforms collect and analyze data about known threats. MISP (Malware Information Sharing Platform) and Recorded Future aggregate Indicators of Compromise (IOCs), providing actionable insights.

Sandboxing for Malware Analysis
Sandboxes provide isolated environments to execute suspicious files and observe their behavior. For example:

Cuckoo Sandbox: Dynamically analyzes executables to detect malicious activity without risking live systems.
These tools work in unison to provide layered security, addressing multiple attack vectors.

5. Incident Response Framework
An effective incident response plan ensures that when an attack occurs, the organization can respond swiftly and decisively, minimizing damage and downtime.

Phases of Incident Response
Identification: Quickly determine the nature, scope, and origin of the threat. For instance, identifying a ransomware variant through its encryption patterns and ransom note format.

Containment: Isolate compromised systems to prevent the attack from spreading. Thi may include disabling accounts, blocking network access, and halting affected processes.

Eradication and Recovery: Remove malware, close exploited vulnerabilities, and restore affected systems using clean backups.

Role of Playbooks
Predefined playbooks outline step-by-step actions for specific attack scenarios, such as phishing, ransomware, or insider threats. These documents standardize responses and ensure rapid action.

6. Proactive Prevention Strategies
While detection and mitigation are vital, proactive prevention reduces the likelihood of advanced attacks succeeding.

Patch Management

Regularly updating software and systems ensures that known vulnerabilities are closed. Tools like WSUS for Windows or Ansible for automated updates streamline this process.

User Education
Human error remains a significant factor in cybersecurity breaches. Training employees to recognize phishing attempts, avoid clicking on suspicious links, and follow best practices strengthens the organization's overall security posture.

Network Segmentation
Segmenting the network into isolated zones restricts attackers' movement. For example:

Placing IoT devices in separate VLANs.
Limiting access to sensitive databases only to authorized personnel.
7. Post-Attack Analysis and Reporting
After an attack, organizations must analyze the incident thoroughly to identify weaknesses and prevent future occurrences.

Comprehensive Reporting
Documenting every aspect of the attack—how it occurred, its impact, and the response—provides valuable insights for stakeholders and regulatory compliance.

Vulnerability Assessment
Conduct a detailed assessment using tools like Nessus or Qualys to identify and address gaps in the security infrastructure.

Continuous Improvement
Implement lessons learned to refine security policies, update configurations, and enhance training programs.

Conclusion
Advanced attacks pose a significant challenge to organizations worldwide. By employing advanced behavioral analysis, leveraging state-of-the-art detection tools, and establishing robust incident response frameworks, organizations can not only detect and mitigate these threats but also build a proactive defense. Continuous improvement and a commitment to best practices ensure resilience against the ever-evolving cyber threat landscape.

Chapter 17: Advanced Ethical Hacking and the Art of Penetration Testing
Introduction
Advanced ethical hacking is a cornerstone of modern cybersecurity, combining technical prowess, analytical skills, and creativity to uncover vulnerabilities before malicious actors can exploit them. Penetration testing (or pentesting) serves as the practical application of this discipline, replicating real-world attack scenarios to evaluate an organization's security posture. This chapter delves into advanced penetration testing methodologies, providing an expanded and detailed exploration of techniques, tools, and processes, from initial planning to mitigation strategies.

1. Planning the Penetration Test
A successful penetration test begins with meticulous planning. Proper preparation aligns testing activities with organizational goals, ensures legal compliance, and sets the stage for accurate and actionable results.

Defining Objectives
Objectives dictate the scope and focus of the penetration test. These could range from assessing the resilience of a web application to evaluating the security of an entire enterprise network. Key considerations include:

Granular Definition: For example, the objective may specify: "Evaluate if sensitive data in the customer database is accessible through unauthorized API calls."
Outcome Expectations: Define metrics, such as the number of vulnerabilities identified, the duration required to compromise the system, or the percentage of critical assets protected.
Thoroughly defined objectives ensure the test remains focused and measurable, avoiding scope creep and delivering actionable insights.

Determining the Scope
The scope sets the boundaries for the test. A comprehensive scope might include:

Systems: Cloud resources, on-premises servers, or IoT devices.
Processes: Internal access controls or third-party integrations.
Exclusions: Critical production systems or resources with operational sensitivities.
For example, testing might exclude sensitive customer-facing systems during peak business hours to prevent service disruptions.

Legal and Ethical Frameworks
Compliance with legal and ethical standards is crucial. Ethical hackers should:

Draft and sign Rules of Engagement (RoE) documents specifying authorized activities and operational boundaries.
Obtain written consent from stakeholders before beginning any testing activities.
Adhere to industry standards like OWASP or ISO 27001 to ensure professionalism and consistency.
2. Advanced Information Gathering
Information gathering (reconnaissance) is the backbone of penetration testing. This phase builds a detailed understanding of the target environment using a combination of passive and active techniques.

Open Source Intelligence (OSINT)
OSINT involves collecting publicly available information about the target using:

Search Engines: Tools like Google Dorking can uncover hidden directories, unindexed pages, or misconfigured APIs.
Tools: Platforms like Shodan identify exposed devices, while Maltego visualizes relationships between domains, emails, and other entities.
Social Media Mining: Extract employee names, organizational hierarchy, or potential phishing targets.
For instance, a tester may uncover a public Git repository with hardcoded credentials during an OSINT investigation.

Active Enumeration
This technique directly interacts with the target environment to identify exploitable weaknesses:

Port Scanning: Use tools like Nmap to identify open ports and services, e.g., a MySQL database running on port 3306.
Service Enumeration: Tools like Netcat or Banner Grabbing reveal software versions, which can be cross-referenced against known vulnerabilities.
DNS Analysis: Tools like Sublist3r enumerate subdomains that could expose less-secured services.
By combining OSINT and active enumeration, testers create a comprehensive blueprint of the target.

3. Vulnerability Scanning and Manual Testing
This phase involves uncovering vulnerabilities that could be exploited to

compromise the system.

Automated Vulnerability Scanning
Automated tools like Nessus, OpenVAS, and Acunetix are used to:

Detect outdated software.
Identify misconfigurations, such as default credentials or open directories.
Highlight exploitable CVEs (Common Vulnerabilities and Exposures).
For example, a scan may reveal a web server running Apache 2.2, which is no longer
supported and vulnerable to remote code execution.

Manual Vulnerability Testing
Manual testing addresses limitations in automated scans by leveraging human
intuition:

Input Validation Testing: Modify user input fields to detect injection flaws or
bypass authentication mechanisms.
API Manipulation: Intercept API calls with tools like Burp Suite to test for
improper authorization or data leakage.
Business Logic Flaws: Identify weaknesses in the way processes are implemented,
such as approval systems missing proper validation.
Manual testing ensures deeper coverage and identifies subtle vulnerabilities missed
by automated tools.

4. Exploitation: Executing Advanced Attacks
This phase demonstrates the impact of identified vulnerabilities by actively
exploiting them.

Buffer Overflow Exploits
Buffer overflows are sophisticated attacks where excess data overwrites critical
memory, allowing attackers to execute arbitrary code. Tools like Metasploit
simplify this process by automating payload delivery.

Example: Exploiting a buffer overflow in an outdated application to gain a reverse
shell on the server.

Privilege Escalation
Privilege escalation leverages misconfigurations or software flaws to elevate
access rights:

Vertical Escalation: A non-privileged user gains administrative access by
exploiting poorly configured SUID files in Linux.
Horizontal Escalation: An attacker assumes the identity of another user by
exploiting insecure session management.
Lateral Movement
After gaining a foothold, attackers explore other parts of the network. Techniques
include:

Extracting stored credentials using Mimikatz.
Exploiting shared drives to spread malware or exfiltrate data.
5. Post-Exploitation Analysis
Post-exploitation focuses on understanding the depth and implications of the
breach.

Data Discovery
Ethical hackers identify and assess valuable data, such as:

Personally identifiable information (PII).
Sensitive configuration files.

Encryption keys or certificates stored insecurely.
Persistence Mechanisms
Establishing persistence mimics how real attackers maintain access:

Backdoors: Create secondary access methods.
Rootkits: Modify kernel processes to evade detection.
Impact Assessment
This involves calculating the potential damage of the compromise, including:

Financial implications.
Reputational risks.
Compliance violations.
6. Reporting and Recommendations
Clear and actionable reporting is the culmination of a penetration test.

Technical Documentation
Provide detailed, reproducible findings:

Vulnerability descriptions.
Evidence of exploitation, such as screenshots or payload execution logs.
Severity ratings based on CVSS (Common Vulnerability Scoring System).
Mitigation Strategies
Offer tailored remediation steps, such as:

"Update Apache to version 2.4.54 to address CVE-YYYY-12345."
"Implement multi-factor authentication for all privileged accounts."
Executive Summary
Translate technical findings into business language, emphasizing risks and the
value of mitigations to stakeholders.

7. Continuous Ethical Hacking and Automation
In a dynamic threat landscape, penetration testing must evolve into a continuous
security process.

Automated Pentesting
Tools like OWASP ZAP integrate with CI/CD pipelines to identify vulnerabilities in
real-time during software development.

Red and Blue Team Collaboration
Ethical hacking thrives in a collaborative ecosystem:

Red Team: Simulates attacks to identify weaknesses.
Blue Team: Fortifies defenses based on insights from simulated breaches.
Purple Teaming
Purple teaming enhances security by merging red and blue team strategies into a
unified defense-testing approach.

Conclusion
Advanced ethical hacking demands a meticulous, methodical approach supported by
sophisticated tools and strategies. From reconnaissance to post-exploitation
reporting, penetration testing offers a comprehensive evaluation of an
organization's defenses. By integrating continuous testing, automating
vulnerability assessments, and fostering a collaborative security culture,
organizations can stay ahead of evolving threats, ensuring robust protection for
their systems and data.

Chapter 18: Advanced Monitoring and Analysis of System Processes
Introduction
Advanced monitoring of system processes forms a cornerstone in cybersecurity and

operational management, especially in complex IT environments. This approach goes beyond basic anomaly detection, encompassing deep contextual understanding, workflow analysis, and preemptive threat mitigation. By identifying vulnerabilities and addressing threats proactively, organizations can safeguard their infrastructure and maintain smooth operations. This chapter delves into comprehensive methodologies, tools, and techniques for advanced monitoring and analysis of processes on Windows and Linux platforms, offering practical insights and detailed examples.

1. The Importance of Monitoring System Processes
Monitoring system processes is an indispensable activity in modern organizations, underpinning security, operational efficiency, and regulatory compliance.

Security
Processes running within a system are often targeted by malicious actors. Monitoring them enables early detection of activities like malware disguising itself as legitimate processes or unauthorized attempts to access sensitive data.

Example: A process with an unexpected name, consuming large amounts of memory and attempting external connections, could signal a cryptojacking attack.
Significance: By promptly identifying and analyzing such processes, administrators can mitigate risks before they escalate into full-blown security breaches.
Performance Optimization
Unchecked processes can lead to inefficient use of resources, causing bottlenecks and reducing overall system performance. Monitoring ensures that resources like CPU, memory, and I/O bandwidth are distributed optimally.

Scenario: Monitoring tools can detect a background process monopolizing CPU resources, enabling administrators to investigate and terminate or reprioritize it.
Result: Enhanced efficiency and minimized risk of service disruptions.
Compliance
Regulations such as GDPR, HIPAA, and PCI DSS mandate detailed logging and tracking of system activities to protect data and maintain transparency.

Requirement: Logs must capture critical events, including process creation, termination, and modifications, ensuring audit readiness.
Compliance Benefit: Proper monitoring demonstrates adherence to legal and regulatory standards, avoiding fines and reputational damage.
2. Advanced Tools for Monitoring Processes
Effective process monitoring hinges on leveraging specialized tools designed for deep visibility and actionable insights. Several advanced utilities are indispensable for this purpose.

Windows Process Monitor (ProcMon)
ProcMon provides real-time tracking of system interactions, including file access, registry changes, and network communications.

Use Case: Identify a rogue process accessing protected registry keys or launching unauthorized network requests.
Features:
Filtering capabilities to isolate specific processes.
Detailed logs for forensic analysis.
Linux Tools: Top and Htop
Top and Htop are powerful tools for monitoring processes on Linux systems, with Htop offering a user-friendly, interactive interface.

Capabilities:
View and sort processes based on resource consumption.
Terminate, suspend, or reprioritize processes directly within the interface.

Example: Htop can help detect a zombie process lingering in the system, enabling efficient cleanup.

SIEM Platforms
Security Information and Event Management (SIEM) platforms such as Splunk and ELK Stack aggregate, analyze, and visualize data from multiple sources, aiding in the detection of complex patterns.

Example: SIEM can correlate login attempts across multiple servers, flagging a potential brute-force attack spanning the network.
Benefits: Centralized logging and advanced threat correlation.

Sysdig and Wireshark
These tools extend monitoring into advanced realms:

Sysdig: Focuses on detailed system calls and network communication monitoring.
Use Case: Detect a process attempting unauthorized data exfiltration.
Wireshark: Specializes in packet-level network analysis.
Example: Identify a compromised process communicating with an unusual IP address.

3. Advanced Monitoring Techniques
Sophisticated monitoring goes beyond routine observations, employing cutting-edge techniques to detect and prevent threats effectively.

Behavioral Profiling
Establishing behavioral baselines for legitimate processes helps detect deviations that might indicate compromise.

Scenario: A database service known to handle local queries begins communicating with external IP addresses, signaling a potential data breach.
Approach: Employ machine learning models to continuously refine these baselines an detect nuanced anomalies.

Real-Time Monitoring
Tools like Nagios and Zabbix provide real-time alerts for anomalies.

Example: Setting a threshold for CPU usage at 80% and receiving alerts when a process consistently exceeds this limit.
Advantage: Immediate awareness enables quicker responses, reducing downtime and potential damage.

Log Analysis
Logs are a treasure trove of information, offering a historical record of process activities.

Windows Example: Use Event Viewer to identify patterns of failed login attempts an investigate further.
Linux Example: Analyze /var/log/messages for abnormal process-related entries.

Process Isolation
Isolating critical processes within containers or virtualized environments mitigates risks.

Example: Use Docker to sandbox potentially vulnerable applications, ensuring that even if a compromise occurs, the threat is contained.

4. Mitigating Threats Through Monitoring
Once anomalies are identified, timely and effective mitigation strategies are essential to neutralize threats and protect the system.

Terminating Malicious Processes
Tools like Task Manager (Windows) and kill (Linux) enable administrators to terminate suspicious processes.

Best Practice: Analyze the process's origin and behavior before termination to avoid disrupting legitimate operations.

Quarantining Affected Files
Malicious processes often leave behind modified or corrupted files. Isolating these files is critical to prevent further damage.

Example: Employ endpoint detection and response (EDR) tools to quarantine files associated with the malicious process.
System Hardening
Implement additional security measures, such as:

Restricting access to critical files and directories.
Enforcing security policies like SELinux (Linux) or enabling Windows Defender Application Control (WDAC).
Notification and Reporting
Automated notifications streamline incident response.

Example: Configure SIEM to send immediate alerts to administrators when a process attempts unauthorized access to sensitive resources.
5. Case Study: Detecting and Mitigating Persistent Malware
Scenario
An organization experienced unexplained performance degradation across critical servers. Sysdig revealed an unauthorized process, svhost32.exe, mimicking a legitimate system process.

Analysis
The process exhibited unusual behavior, including high resource consumption and external communication attempts.
Behavioral profiling confirmed that the process was not part of normal operations.
Mitigation
Action: Terminated the process and quarantined all associated files.
Response: Blocked the external IP address via firewall rules.
Prevention: Implemented endpoint monitoring and routine audits to catch similar threats earlier.
Outcome
The organization enhanced its monitoring protocols, reducing its mean time to detect (MTTD) and mean time to respond (MTTR) to similar incidents.

Conclusion
Advanced monitoring and analysis of system processes are integral to ensuring a secure and efficient IT environment. By leveraging sophisticated tools, implementing cutting-edge techniques, and adopting proactive mitigation strategies, organizations can detect and neutralize threats before they escalate. A robust monitoring framework bolstered by detailed analysis and swift action ensures resilience against evolving cybersecurity challenges.

Chapter 19: Hardening Operating Systems – Advanced Approaches and Techniques
Introduction
Operating system (OS) hardening is a foundational practice for safeguarding IT infrastructures from modern cyber threats. The process involves systematically reducing vulnerabilities, removing unnecessary functionalities, and implementing advanced security measures tailored to specific environments like Windows, Linux, or macOS. This chapter provides a comprehensive guide to advanced OS hardening techniques, tools, and methodologies. By employing these strategies, organizations can significantly enhance their systems' resilience against evolving threats.

1. The Essence of Operating System Hardening
What is OS Hardening?
Operating systems often ship with default settings optimized for usability rather than security. Hardening transforms these defaults into a fortified baseline that

minimizes the potential attack surface while maintaining operational functionality.

Key Objectives
Attack Surface Reduction: Disabling unnecessary features or services reduces potential entry points for attackers. For instance, if a system is primarily used as a web server, only essential services like HTTP and HTTPS should be active.
Improved Resilience: Systems with fewer vulnerabilities are harder to exploit, forcing attackers to exert greater effort or abandon their attempts.
Operational Integrity: Hardened systems are better equipped to withstand misconfigurations, accidental changes, or basic exploitation attempts.
Real-World Impact
A public-facing server left with default configurations is an open invitation for attackers. Hardening it by implementing firewalls, restricting access to only required services, and employing strong access controls significantly reduces risks.

2. Fundamental Principles of OS Hardening
Patching and Updates
Keeping systems updated is one of the most critical aspects of hardening. Unpatched software and OS vulnerabilities are a primary vector for cyberattacks.

Automated Updates: Use automated systems like Windows Server Update Services (WSUS) or unattended-upgrades on Linux to streamline patching.
Test Before Deployment: Always test patches in a staging environment to avoid unexpected disruptions in production.
Case Study: The 2017 WannaCry ransomware attack exploited an unpatched SMB vulnerability in Windows systems. Prompt updates could have prevented the attack, which caused billions in damages globally.
Access Control and Principle of Least Privilege
Access control ensures that users and processes have only the permissions necessary for their tasks.

Implement Role-Based Access Control (RBAC): Define granular roles and ensure strict adherence to the least privilege principle. For instance, a database administrator shouldn't have access to financial accounting systems.
Segregation of Duties: Separate critical roles to prevent abuse. For example, an IT administrator shouldn't also handle security auditing.
Administrative Privileges:
Use standard user accounts for daily tasks.
Restrict administrative privileges to specific accounts and enforce multifactor authentication (MFA) for access.
Disabling Unnecessary Services
Each enabled service is a potential vulnerability. Identifying and disabling unused or redundant services is a cornerstone of hardening.

Audit Services Regularly:
On Linux, use commands like systemctl list-unit-files or chkconfig --list to identify active services.
On Windows, leverage services.msc or PowerShell scripts.
Replace Legacy Services:
Replace Telnet with SSH.
Disable FTP in favor of SFTP.
Best Practice: Enable services only on an as-needed basis and regularly review service logs for anomalies.
Firewall Configuration
Firewalls are critical for controlling inbound and outbound traffic, especially for public-facing systems.

Granular Rule Management:

Allow only specific IP ranges or ports.
Deny all nonessential traffic by default.
Firewall Types:
Windows: Use the Windows Defender Firewall with Advanced Security.
Linux: Implement iptables, nftables, or ufw for robust traffic control.
Example: Block all ports except 22 (SSH), 80 (HTTP), and 443 (HTTPS) for a Linux web server.
Encryption
Encrypting sensitive data ensures its confidentiality, even in the event of unauthorized access.

Disk Encryption:
Windows: BitLocker offers full-disk encryption.
Linux: Use LUKS to encrypt partitions.
macOS: Enable FileVault for disk-level encryption.
Network Encryption:
Enforce TLS 1.2 or higher for web services.
Use VPNs for secure communication between endpoints.
3. Advanced Hardening Techniques for Specific OS Environments
Windows Hardening
Group Policy Objects (GPOs):
Configure account lockout policies to mitigate brute-force attacks.
Enforce password complexity requirements.
Windows Defender Application Control (WDAC):
Restrict executable files to those signed by trusted publishers.
PowerShell Logging:
Enable script logging to detect malicious usage.
Example: Use Set-ExecutionPolicy to restrict script execution.
Linux Hardening
SELinux/AppArmor:
SELinux enforces Mandatory Access Control (MAC), restricting processes to specific roles.
AppArmor profiles define what an application can and cannot do.
Example: Prevent a compromised web server from accessing system directories.
Permission Management:
Set permissions on sensitive files using chmod and chown.
Example: Restrict /etc/shadow to root-only access.
Log Auditing:
Use tools like Auditd to monitor system events and detect unauthorized changes.
macOS Hardening
System Integrity Protection (SIP):
Prevent unauthorized modification of critical system files.
Gatekeeper:
Allow only applications from the Mac App Store or verified developers.
FileVault:
Encrypt the entire disk to protect data from physical theft.
4. Automating the Hardening Process
Tools for Automation
Ansible:
Example Playbook: Disable root login across all Linux servers:
yaml
Copy code

```
- name: Disable SSH root login
  hosts: all
  tasks:
    - lineinfile:
        path: /etc/ssh/sshd_config
        regexp: '^PermitRootLogin'
        line: 'PermitRootLogin no'
```

PowerShell Desired State Configuration (DSC):
Automate the deployment of GPO settings.
SCAP:
Automates compliance checks against CIS Benchmarks or NIST guidelines.
5. Validation and Verification of Hardening
Tools for Validation
Vulnerability Scanning:
Use Nessus or OpenVAS to detect unpatched vulnerabilities or misconfigurations.
Compliance Auditing:
Compare configurations against CIS or DISA benchmarks.
Continuous Monitoring:
Deploy OSSEC to detect unauthorized file or process changes.
Routine Testing
Periodically test hardened systems with penetration testing tools to ensure real-world robustness.
6. Case Study: Hardening a Corporate Data Center
Scenario
A retail company sought to secure its data center after a security audit identified significant risks.

Measures Taken
Disabled legacy services such as Telnet and implemented SSH with MFA.
Applied CIS Level 2 benchmarks for Linux servers, enforcing strict SELinux policies.
Configured VLANs and firewalls to isolate sensitive systems from less secure endpoints.
Outcome
The organization observed a 60% reduction in vulnerabilities, improved compliance with regulatory requirements, and enhanced operational stability.

Conclusion
Operating system hardening is a continuous process that evolves with new threats and technologies. Advanced techniques, combined with automation and rigorous validation, enable organizations to achieve robust security postures. By systematically implementing these strategies, businesses can protect their critical systems from emerging threats while maintaining optimal performance.

Chapter 20: Advanced Monitoring and Continuous Resilience – The Future of Cybersecurity
Introduction
In the ever-changing landscape of cybersecurity, continuous monitoring and resilience have emerged as foundational pillars for safeguarding digital infrastructures. These practices not only involve detecting and mitigating threats but also designing systems capable of maintaining operations despite evolving challenges. This chapter provides an in-depth exploration of advanced monitoring techniques, the integration of artificial intelligence (AI) in cybersecurity, structured incident response frameworks, and strategies for achieving robust resilience.

1. The Importance of Continuous Monitoring
Continuous monitoring ensures real-time oversight of systems, allowing organizations to proactively detect and address potential threats. This dynamic approach replaces static, periodic assessments with an ongoing evaluation of risks and performance.

Proactive Threat Detection
Continuous monitoring identifies anomalies that could signal emerging threats, such as brute-force attacks, malware infiltration, or unauthorized data access.
Example: An unusual volume of outbound data traffic might indicate an attempt at

exfiltrating sensitive information.
Early detection prevents minor incidents from escalating into significant security breaches, providing a first line of defense.
Operational Efficiency
Beyond security, monitoring aids in optimizing system performance by identifying bottlenecks or underutilized resources.
Example: Monitoring resource consumption on virtual machines can ensure that resources are appropriately allocated to critical workloads.
Regulatory Compliance
Compliance with frameworks like GDPR, PCI DSS, and ISO 27001 often requires detailed logging and continuous monitoring of system activities.
Example: Logs tracking access to customer data ensure traceability and support audits.
A well-designed monitoring framework integrates seamlessly with an organization's IT infrastructure, balancing security, performance, and compliance requirements.

2. Tools for Advanced Monitoring and Analysis
Effective monitoring relies on sophisticated tools capable of processing large datasets and offering actionable insights. These tools enable centralized oversight and facilitate informed decision-making.

Splunk
Splunk collects, analyzes, and visualizes data from various sources, offering a centralized platform for log management and threat detection.
Example Use: Configuring Splunk to detect multiple failed login attempts across systems and triggering alerts for potential brute-force attacks.
Elastic Stack (ELK)
This open-source suite includes Elasticsearch, Logstash, and Kibana, providing powerful data indexing, processing, and visualization capabilities.
Example Use: Using Kibana dashboards to monitor network traffic patterns and identify deviations indicative of Distributed Denial of Service (DDoS) attacks.
OSSEC
A host-based intrusion detection system (HIDS) that monitors log files, configuration changes, and user activities in real-time.
Example Use: Detecting unauthorized modifications to critical system files and sending automated alerts.
AI-Powered Solutions
Machine learning and AI are revolutionizing monitoring by identifying nuanced patterns of abnormal activity.
Example Use: Tools like Darktrace build a behavioral baseline and autonomously flag activities deviating from normal operations.
These tools collectively enhance situational awareness, empowering organizations to detect and address security incidents efficiently.

3. Integrating AI and Automation in Cybersecurity
The integration of AI and automation into cybersecurity transforms the way organizations identify and mitigate threats, offering faster and more accurate responses.

Advanced Threat Detection
Anomaly Identification: Machine learning algorithms analyze historical data to flag behaviors that deviate from established norms.
Example: Recognizing a spike in file downloads from a sensitive database during non-working hours as a potential insider threat.
Automated Response Systems
AI-driven systems like SOAR (Security Orchestration, Automation, and Response) automate repetitive security tasks, such as isolating compromised systems or revoking access to breached accounts.
Example: Automatically blocking an IP address attempting repeated unauthorized

access to the internal network.
Enhanced Threat Intelligence
AI enhances threat intelligence by correlating data from multiple sources,
identifying attack vectors, and recommending preventive measures.
Example: Identifying that a specific vulnerability has been exploited across
multiple endpoints and prioritizing its patching.
AI and automation enable faster decision-making, reducing human error and improvin
the overall security posture of an organization.

4. Building a Resilient System
Resilience is not just about preventing attacks; it's about ensuring that systems
can recover swiftly and maintain functionality under duress. A resilient
infrastructure is prepared for both known and unforeseen challenges.

Network Segmentation
Dividing the network into isolated segments limits the movement of attackers and
protects critical assets.
Example: Placing financial systems in a secured segment isolated from user
workstations to prevent lateral attacks.
Backup and Disaster Recovery
Regular backups are essential for resilience, ensuring data restoration in case of
ransomware or hardware failure.
Best Practice: Implement offsite or air-gapped backups that remain inaccessible to
malware.
High Availability and Redundancy
Designing systems with failover capabilities ensures continuous service during
disruptions.
Example: Deploying redundant database clusters that seamlessly transfer operations
in the event of a node failure.
By combining these strategies, organizations can minimize downtime and maintain
business continuity even during severe incidents.

5. Structuring an Incident Response Plan
An effective incident response plan ensures that organizations can manage security
breaches systematically and minimize their impact.

Phases of Incident Response
Preparation:
Develop response protocols, assign roles, and conduct regular training simulations
Example: Running a ransomware attack simulation to test the readiness of the
response team.
Detection and Analysis:
Use monitoring tools to detect incidents and assess their scope.
Example: Analyzing firewall logs to identify the origin and extent of a DDoS
attack.
Containment:
Isolate affected systems to prevent further damage.
Example: Disconnecting compromised endpoints from the network to stop malware
propagation.
Eradication:
Remove malicious software or unauthorized access points.
Example: Deploying updated antivirus definitions to clean infected systems.
Recovery:
Restore operations using clean backups and secure configurations.
Example: Rebuilding a compromised server using a verified image and applying
updated patches.
Post-Mortem:
Document lessons learned and update security policies to address gaps.
Example: Revising access controls to prevent future insider threats.

A comprehensive plan ensures that incidents are addressed effectively and that the organization emerges stronger from each challenge.

6. The Future of Resilience in Cybersecurity

As cyber threats continue to evolve, so must the strategies organizations use to defend against them. Future trends in resilience emphasize adaptability, collaboration, and cutting-edge technologies.

Emerging Trends

Cyber Threat Intelligence (CTI):
Leveraging global intelligence sources to predict and counteract emerging threats.
Example: Blocking IP ranges associated with known malicious actors using CTI feeds.

Zero Trust Architecture:
Treating every access request as untrusted until verified, even within the network perimeter.
Example: Implementing multifactor authentication (MFA) for all internal systems.

Quantum-Resistant Cryptography:
Preparing for the advent of quantum computing by adopting encryption algorithms resistant to quantum attacks.

These innovations underscore the importance of staying ahead of adversaries through continuous learning and adaptation.

Conclusion

Continuous monitoring and resilience are integral to modern cybersecurity frameworks, enabling organizations to detect threats in real time, respond efficiently, and recover swiftly. By integrating AI, automating responses, and designing robust systems, businesses can navigate the complexities of the evolving threat landscape. The future of cybersecurity lies not only in preventing breaches but also in ensuring that systems remain functional and secure under the most challenging circumstances.

Final Book Conclusion

This book has explored the multifaceted world of cybersecurity, offering insights into threat landscapes, advanced defenses, and strategies for resilience. From understanding malware to hardening systems, monitoring processes, and fostering a culture of security awareness, the journey outlined here equips readers with the knowledge and tools to face modern challenges confidently.

Cybersecurity is a continuous journey of innovation, vigilance, and adaptation. By leveraging the lessons in this book, professionals can contribute to a safer digital future, protecting not just systems and data but also the people and organizations that rely on them.